MAKE THEM REMEMBER YOU

LIVE YOUR LEGACY NOW

VIRGIL BRANNON

MAKE THEM REMEMBER YOU
LIVE YOUR LEGACY NOW

iUniverse books may be ordered through booksellers or by contacting:

iUniverse
1663 Liberty Drive
Bloomington, IN 47403
www.iuniverse.com
1-800-Authors (1-800-288-4677)

Because of the dynamic nature of the Internet, any web addresses or links contained in this book may have changed since publication and may no longer be valid. The views expressed in this work are solely those of the author and do not necessarily reflect the views of the publisher, and the publisher hereby disclaims any responsibility for them.

Any people depicted in stock imagery provided by Getty Images are models, and such images are being used for illustrative purposes only.
Certain stock imagery © Getty Images.

ISBN: 978-1-5320-6599-6 (sc)
ISBN: 978-1-5320-6601-6 (hc)
ISBN: 978-1-5320-6600-9 (e)

Library of Congress Control Number: 2019901798

Print information available on the last page.

iUniverse rev. date: 02/26/2019

This book in dedicated to Austin and Justice.
Sons do not come any better than the two of you.

CONTENTS

ABOUT THE AUTHOR

Virgil Brannon is the founder of I AM VISION INC., a nonprofit youth program. The mission of I AM VISION INC. is to embrace and empower youth by challenging them to boost their vision via hands-on opportunities and encouraging their determination to excel in life. Virgil's overall effort is to promote young people's growth and their ability to dream and envision success to develop their leadership and academic capabilities.

However, his charitable heart is with the empowerment of young people seeking positive mentors to help them navigate challenging obstacles. Virgil's career background is also in private investigations and legal support, marketing, music management, and consulting.

To better serve youth and their families, Virgil attended Shepherd's Care Bible College and received a dual master's and doctorate of ministry in religious counseling so that he would be equipped to address vital issues associated with socioeconomically disadvantaged youth and their families.

Virgil didn't stop there. He embraced a large number of business and socially based courses so that he could make certain that his organization was just as business savvy as it was charitably focused. These efforts resulted in not only master's and doctoral degrees but an astonishing concentration of social enterprise. Today, you can find Virgil with his hands in a number of business deals that generate funding to support his endeavors to make it a little easier for youth to reach their full potential.

PREFACE

Make Them Remember You! was written to focus on our purpose in life. It is intended as a spiritual guide to embrace the positive over the negative that we face every day. I wrote it to show readers how much we matter to the world and how important it is for us to challenge ourselves. It was written to explain how we are the beneficiaries and the inheritors of our ancestors, no matter what they endured or suffered, and not a burden, for better or worse. It was written to show that although the Creator blessed all of us, we have to learn what to do with those blessings. The book will empower readers to go forward in living happier lives while it offers solutions and simple ways for us to make our lives better. The aim is to present information that will be relatable, informative, and interesting. I hope it inspires and boosts readers' confidence to do more with their lives. At the same time, I want to bring a better perspective to why it is so important to stop complaining about bad events that happened so far in the past that cannot help us today. Unless we know what to do with that knowledge, these problems will still bloom. I hope readers will see and understand the importance of the basic knowledge we learned in school and how it transforms our lives.

I wrote the book to show how there is no limitation to what we can do and that nothing holds one back but oneself. *Make Them Remember You!* will give those who do not know their purpose a fresh start, a second chance, or a new beginning. The book will show them who they are and why they matter and then offer solutions for how to change their lives for the better.

I hope readers will discover how unlimited the sky is to them; what their roles and responsibilities are; and how we must become better at controlling our own lives, our destinies, and, most importantly, our individual selves.

As we make corrections, we must understand how we arrived at this point where we have failed to apply and celebrate our ancestors' accomplishments and instead applied and assumed their suffering. We are not savage beasts, slaves, murderers, rapists, and fools. Our ancestors were doctors, lawyers, engineers, designers, scientists, mathematicians, writers, builders, and other great human beings, and so are you. We are the beneficiaries of the past, and all we have today is our inheritance. The key to life is growth, and everything must progress. We cannot take life for granted and spend too much time talking about oppressive and depressing things we cannot change. And we cannot be something we have never lived, let alone experienced. How can we be affected by something if we were never there? This type of teaching and constant indoctrination about the past limits your thinking and progress; holds you back; and comes from those who have an agenda to separate you from your gifts, talents, and other human beings.

The burden lies on those who have restricted you. It's time that we take things seriously because we have been purposely distracted and not shown what to do with the Creator's work. The solution rests at the basic level of learning.

Many of us have grown to believe that several academic subjects are not needed in the real world. We believe addition and subtraction have no real uses, other than to count money. We believe language is just about learning how to read. Many believe history and science have no value because history is about someone else's past and science is just about animals, plants, and body parts. These four basic activities are the primary tools we need to achieve success if they are taught as I see them. There are two parts to success: first you get the lesson, and then you must apply it. Many of us were not taught how to apply them and use those subjects to survive, where to look to see them play out, or how to make the corrections when we failed so the worst of history will not repeat itself through us. One of the main reasons many of us thought we would never need those subjects is that we were never taught how to apply them, find ourselves in one or more of them, and nurture our gifts or talents in them.

As we move forward to make the correction, my hope is that we will stop dwelling on the past and instead learn how to forgive, get up, and go get what is waiting for us. It's time. Make them remember you! Go get it and live your legacy now.

INTRODUCTION

Education has changed our society as if we are a social experiment. It seems like we are guinea pigs in labs, running in circles trying to find the nearest exit to set us free. It has gone from what God wants us to know to what politicians plan for us to know. This agenda they have planned creates division between us and separates the haves from the have-nots and blacks from whites. This agenda makes one believe they have no purpose. If we believe in success, why are we showing envy and jealousy toward one another? These are two of the sins we were told to avoid.

For far too long they have had us sitting around complaining about what others have done to better themselves. We complain that they make too much money, are only out for themselves, and don't want the rest of us to succeed. Continuing to complain as they would want us to will not help us! Whatever hard work people put in to acquire wealth, they deserve it. Whatever they decide to buy for themselves with their money is rightfully theirs. We have to stop complaining about someone else's moment in their story. For us to advance in life, we must first learn what has not advanced us and then search for what will change that.

Every year, we are losing thousands of our young people because they don't know who they are and their purpose. Our youth are losing their lives to gun violence, drug addiction, sex trafficking, suicide, gang affiliation, teen pregnancy, dropping out of school, and the breakdown of family structure because most of them do not know who they are, do not see their self-worth, and have not yet found their purpose. Children today are lost without a recognizable alternative or another way to envision life. Out of all that they are taught, many of them believe they will never use that knowledge after finishing school. Other times, they cannot see or understand what the material has to do with them or their future. Many are lost because we are not tending to their needs, showing them the way, and passing a legacy of values down to them.

With almost 70 percent of African American households headed by single mothers, 51 percent of our youths without jobs to occupy their time and minds, and 20 percent of kids graduating from high school not ready for college, these tragedies will continue to happen. These children do not know that greatness is within them. They do not know the Creator passed down a legacy to our ancestors and that now it lies with us to pass it down to them. Adding to these problems is an outrageous number of fathers who continue to abandon their responsibility of making day-to-day corrections in their children's lives. These fathers are not living up to their ancestors' legacy by making their own future generation's life better. Instead, many of them react violently and become criminals because they are lost. Homes with no fathers are destructive and worsened when the controlling government comes and seeks total control over the family, becoming the parental guardian after forcing the fathers out.

One of our biggest failures was allowing the removal of God's name and prayer from American public schools just to bring comfort to others who are not from this country. But that, too, is our problem. We all should know God and His work. The inability of students to learn what the Creator wants from them has made them more chaotic, confused, and lost. Today, many of the lost and confused are not afraid of committing the same crime or worse. Some of them later become repeat offenders with no chance to get ahead because they are not sure of themselves and their creative purpose.

For the last four decades, we have failed to approach this problem correctly, and as a result, we have the same problems today, although they are worse because no one is willing to take responsibility and challenge the status quo. The government decided to take matters into its own hands, creating programs that do not work. The government did not create a program that teaches young people how to apply to life what they learn in school. Although it put bandages on the problem, it did not solve it. It gave us gang prevention and conflict resolution, which helps some gang members understand some of their problems and maybe later get jobs, but it has never elevated them out of poverty, away from their neighborhood, or from the problem completely. It gave us Scared Straight, a program that allows kids to visit a correctional institution to experience a fast-forward view of the consequences of criminal behavior, but it never shows them what to do or how to find their greatness. As a result, many of them have become the exact image of the inmates meant to scare them. With no alternative to change their environment, many youth find comfort in the scare because they cannot find a straighter path to succeed. The government also gave us Job Corps, but it failed because most of the kids could not find jobs. The government even claimed to stop teen pregnancy through Planned Parenthood, birth control, and the passing out of condoms. But that plan placed us on three sides—death for the innocent, jail for the runaway fathers, and then life in poverty for many single mothers without help from those fathers.

The government has become too big. It interferes with our lives in many ways and has been ineffective in addressing a vast host of social issues.

These problems cause us to go through life depressed, stressed, anxious, uptight, and on the edge. Understand that at that point many of us do not recognize we are sick but have the potential to be great. We lose our jobs or loved ones, go into poverty, have financial challenges, live in uncomfortable environments, and more. But whatever that sickness is, it has turned a person into a patient, and if not treated correctly, this problem will lead to a life of chaos and destruction passed down to other generations. No matter what environment or background we come from, we are all at risk if we don't know our purpose. Life is decided by how we think and react to challenges, but it is best that we take responsibility and think many times before complaining and taking action.

Everyone has suffered from a tragedy, but the key is to get back on track. It's time to live our legacy and chase our dreams and not be rolling around in the suffering someone planned for us. We are not slaves anymore or living in captivity. We have to stop living our ancestors' suffering and start living their successes and accomplishments, to become the heirs and the beneficiaries of their contributions and turn the negative into positive. We need to finish where they left off so our children and their children will have something to take to the next level and build upon. It's time to advance toward a good life so children and their parents will not become confused and misled. Many of the misled were never taught how important their lives really are to the world. If many of us had known better, we would have done greater things. If we had known from the start how to make the best decisions, life would be a lot easier.

So I ask the question, When do we learn about the Creator's work and what He might want us to know? If we knew, many of us would be further along in our American experience by now. And if we had been taught what we were told not to do—what we could achieve—what seems unreachable would be in our possession right now.

But this is our problem now as much as it is theirs. Nothing can hold us back once we know the truth. So how long are we going to complain?

Understand that your life and legacy did not start during a massacre, genocide, slavery, or holocaust. You were great many years before that time.

We can achieve life success through faith in God, a desire to let go of the past, and a willingness to embrace the good in life instead of wallowing in the negativity that breeds bad social behavior. It's time we take our thinking to the next level to understand how blessed we are and what is blocking us from succeeding. If the problem was started by the government coming into your life, claiming to help by creating laws to restrict you, why do you think more interference by the government and more laws can solve your problem? We cannot expect government schools to teach us everything.

So how do we solve these problems? How do we get the message to those who do not know they were born great? How do we get them to know there is no limit to what they can do and become? *Make Them Remember You!* will teach just that—how to find your purpose, follow your dreams and live your legacy, the one our ancestors intended for us to have and live out.

Join me as we go back to the basics, and imagine if you could see life through the vision of the Creator and what He might want us to know. We go back to academic studies and observe what we missed. We reintroduce them in a way that allows us to gain a clear understanding of our lives and our purpose, who we are, and what we can become. Would there be more success? Yes! Imagine if academic studies—science, math, history, and language—were presented to help you envision your life in the right way.

We all must understand that each of us is the best we have! But we must take responsibility, stop complaining, go after our dreams, and start living our legacy, the one that the Creator and others who came before left us.

This book is that lesson, a book of application on how to find yourself and your purpose using the Creator's basic lessons. This book will teach you the basics for academia and what we need to know to succeed. A great start is by thinking—outside the box!—and asking questions to understand the core of life. *Make Them Remember You!* will show you who you are and your purpose. It will explain how to see far beyond a present of low expectations, and in the same process, you will learn your purpose. So I ask you to follow me on this journey as we take history, language, science, and math, one after the other, and apply them to life.

Part 1
The Legacy

Make Them Remember You

ONE

History

What we learned in school about history is what people did long before our time. We learned who those people were and what they may have contributed. I remember as far back as the sixth grade hearing many of my classmates say to the teacher, "Why are we learning about history? We will never use it." That thought came from how the teachers were instructed to teach history to us, which left out what we do with the information afterward. All we received was a history lesson, not how we apply it to our lives.

Living Legacy

The nature of a legacy is something of great value, whether a gift, money, property, special information, or documents that you can pass down to someone and that could benefit him or her in the future. In most cases, it's handed down so you will be remembered long after you have moved on to another life. Often, it's giving to a family member or close friend to make their life a little easier or to avoid having to struggle or suffer any hardship in establishing themselves in the future. Individuals who receive something are the beneficiaries, the inheritors of a legacy.

For years we have been told that history is "the study of the past as it relates to human beings," but that is not so true. The truth about history is in stories of the Creator—our time of existence in the present with Him, as told in the future. History—the past—is just how it appears. When you take the word *history* and divide it in two, you will get "His-story" but from our story. It is His-story with us in it. All of us have a chapter in His-story. Each of us has one to tell, but it is not history until it is in the past. There is no story or His-story without human beings; we must be here to tell it. There is great power in history when you learn how to use it. History is a collection of our stories—our walk, journey, work, memories, and experiences while we are here on this earth with the Creator. It tells the work of the Creator and our efforts, trials, and tribulations of surviving while searching to find ourselves and our unique abilities.

History is about time, building our legacy, and passing down whatever we possess of great value to our children. It tells of our individual journeys, leaving our marks and letting those we do not know understand who we are. "Make them remember you." The Creator did just that—He made us remember Him, and as it is written, in the beginning of time when there was no such thing as man, it was only the Creator. He created or brought forward all things to form what has become His legacy—His-story and our stories. Over time, He made all things come to pass, but only for their purpose to have a future. He then made man a part of that history to become the one who would first live and then later tell His-story and how He existed to them. History is all our stories combined to create His-story, but He requires all of us to tell them. Within those stories, there are different versions about what happened to individuals in their present time when they had breath, lived, and walked the earth. It is in those stories that the Creator gave all of us plenty of time to live out a story and the opportunity to find our purpose on our journey.

Each person was given a path to travel, a lifespan of almost a hundred years to live, enough time to find his or her gifts, talents, or unique abilities. One hundred years is about the highest age we typically get to live on earth, exploring our purpose and later using those gifts, talents, or unique abilities to make a living for our family and ourselves. During those times, the Creator tests us and blesses us before He advances us. Many of us are blessed with a gift, whereas others seek to discover a talent. Let it be known that a talent is something we practice or develop, and that over time, we become good at. Often it shows in those who are determined, ambitious, and motivated.

In contrast, a gift is just as it sounds: something given to you without costing you anything. But it can be taken away if it is never used. Gifts are passed down from one person to the next. It is one's inheritance. It comes in many forms. Greatness is in your DNA, and I challenge all of you to use it. Dream big! Many of us are given our gifts early in life, so we have no problem finding ourselves. A good example of that is a person who is blessed with a gift of running with tremendous speed and, later with training, uses that speed to run track, play soccer, or steal bases for a baseball team. So if you want to change your life, it is in you to do so. The brain is like a computer. They both have to be programmed, but you have to program it to make what is genuinely unique about you come forward and with the right decisions. You can solve your own problem if you program your brain or your thinking to find your genius. There are simple ways to program our brains positively, as opposed to negatively. I will go into more details throughout the book, but mainly in chapter 8.

Once you find your genius, you will find your gift or talent. Your genius is what you have or can do that is difficult for others but easy for you. The solution is in you. The schools will not and cannot teach us about our self and our purpose. Teachers in a classroom will not teach you your genius; the curriculum is set up to deprogram that. Plus there is not enough time in a school day for one teacher to teach each student his or her genius. The educational system does not want too many geniuses; it wants to make sure there will be enough people to carry out geniuses' ideas. So you must learn outside of school how to tap into your genius. Regardless of the gift, each is a blessing advanced after being tested by the Creator.

His Time

Understand that before man, there had never been a need for time, to reference it or to have something called "history." The only reason time exists is for human beings to record the events of their journey and their walk to understand their purpose with the Creator. And on that walk or journey, the Creator gives us blessings after testing us. Without time, there would be no story to tell and no need for history or any record of the past to be presented. So when the Creator gave us nights and days, it was only for man to keep track of time, not for Him to use. He has no need to record time. The only reason we even have seasons is so that we can identify the climate conditions of certain events in our lives that take place with Him. All of us have something we did during a spring, summer, winter, and fall, and we all refer to them in telling stories. It does not matter if those stories happened in the hot sun or cold snow; they are in time and in season with the Creator. So we are clearly the witnesses to and narrators of history, and it is important that we remember what happened in His-story. Our assignment is to tell our stories of what we did with the Creator and how He existed to us during our time.

Our walk or journey is of our own time, from the beginning of our lives to death. Our stories tell the sequence that leads us to our destiny and purpose. It is the length of our relationship and time we have spent with the Creator. However, for many, instead of telling God's story, the problem has been that we tell our own without Him in it. Many of the stories we have told have been about material things—what we have and how we look, as though we did things on our own and created or brought them forward ourselves. And as you know now, we did not! We build upon only what we are given and is here for us to use. All of this is why I refer to history as His-story, the story of the Creator. Our stories are a collection of His knowledge, or the study of the Creator's history.

Our main purposes for our story are to explore life, find our unique abilities, and later tell our experience about what He did for us during our time or what we did with Him in His-story. This makes history the story of the Creator and our time of existing with Him.

Each of us is the greatest thing that has ever happened to this world. We are the only ones who can tell others what we have experienced and what we have witnessed others doing. History tells those experiences about how great we are and what we can do to change the future, but only time allows us to perform the task. History defines the time in which all things exist and occur to an individual, but it is time that measures events and how long they last and allows actions to exist.

A story recounts a sequence of events, but it is the narrator who tells the story. All of us are the narrators of history, but it is the Creator who has written and foreseen each one of our stories. These stories—our journeys, walks, experiences, moments, and memories—make up the Creator's history, for He is the author of life and whom history is about, but we write our own ending to our individual story. We are all historians; we are the researchers if we study and know the past. We are the heirs and descendants of historians. Our lives count for His existence because we are the evidence and the witness of them, and as long as we exist, the Creator exists. History does not exist without us because there must be someone here to tell the stories. As long as there have been human beings, the Creator has always existed, especially to those who acknowledge Him.

His-story exists for all, even for the ones who do not believe. So what determines history or becomes a legacy are those things we do today, at this given moment. But understand, it is not history until it is written or happens, so do not waste any of your time.

It is important that we make the best of our time. Before acting, we must know our story to understand who we are, our future, and that time will make a difference in our story and our past if we are not aware of what we do. We can learn from the stories of others' experiences and our own. This will make us more of a contributor than a burden.

History deals with time and how much of it we put into searching for our purpose and leaving our mark. But if you remove all of mankind from the face of this earth, there will be no marks, and time will not exist. So I ask, if it is not your time, then whose time is it if you do not put in work? Who then will tell your story, and what will it say? Oftentimes, those who have told stories have been called storytellers, narrators, or liars. Which one do you want to tell your story? Ever since the beginning, there have been people who have lied while telling another's story, rewriting it to keep the truth from being told. These lying people do not want you to know yourself, your purpose, and His-story. They are not moral people with good values; telling the truth hurts their agenda and stops their experiment to control you.

Relating History to Us

Another way to see history is as a comparison between what happens in the present and the past, or the now and then. In school, history is taught with no comparison and by learning the past only, but that's half the knowledge and information about a subject. Every book you read is a part of His-story and one or more person's story and experiences—what they did or contributed to this world with the Creator. However, today's history classes are not taught this way. Instead, the past is taught with no information about the present. That means students don't learn about how the past relates to them and what has changed. The present is virtually absent, there only in the physical bodies of the students and teacher discussing the past. It is not there for them to even see change. When almost no one includes the work of the present with the past, it becomes harder for students to see the importance of learning history and how it relates to them. If they cannot see their potential or what they can change or improve in the present, history is dead to them.

The history that is taught in school must focus on us. The teaching of history must involve every aspect of oneself to the point where we are the center of attention and the main subject when speaking about or discussing the past. What I believe the Creator wants us to know about history is our role in it. He wants us to know that history is about the present, how things change over time, because nothing can change if there is no story to compare it with so that we can make adjustments or changes. If we cannot picture ourselves in history or imagine ourselves making changes, how will we know our purpose and what is expected of us?

History or His-story must be taught within the context of time and changes and not be limited only to what life was once like or the events that happened. Allowing this comparison enables students in the physical change to be involved with creating new ideas from what we were given. How can change happen if no one in the present will be teaching in the future the difference between this present and that future? The question becomes, What will be our story, and what will it say we did or contributed to make a change in history, in His-story?

Right Now

The most important time in our lives is the present, the right here and right now. That is the time in which we get to make a difference—doing what we love, getting to work on our future, and creating our story. All of us have a past and a future, but to have a story, have a history, or be in His-story, there must be work and a time when the events first take place. The only way we can teach history is by our present happening and then, as it becomes the past, explaining what happened in the beginning to make the present become the past. Someone must record what happened and when, how far people have come, or what has changed over that time to call the events history. It does not matter what the past says about things in history; what does matter and will make a difference is what we do in the present. Since things are constantly changing, the present can never be what it once was. It can only become what it now means in the present; that is the moment when things are being examined, researched, and spoken for. The past can only become history, but the present can be almost anything in the future, as long as we *go get it and Live Our Legacy Now.*

In the instance of the present, the past is not relevant and has no life, because that moment has already been recorded in time. It cannot move or change its position. The past is like a printed book, and once it is written, it is set—frozen, dead, in idle, and immovable. You can read it over and over, but you cannot change it, because the time for doing that has gone by. It is history, the past. We have to move on and stop harboring negative feelings about people who have wronged us. We have to come to grips with our past and accept that what happened cannot be changed. The more we drag out the negative from the past, the more it keeps our children from pursuing their dreams. All it does is make them afraid to step outside their environment because life there is unfamiliar to them. It's hard to be comfortable when we are afraid and a place is unknown to us. This wallowing in the past makes no sense when in pursuit of dreams, because we miss out on opportunities that could change our lives.

It's time to put the past aside so the healing can began. Healing starts by learning how to forgive and putting your focus on living out your legacy. The only way the past can become relevant is by taking a new action in the present to make it a part of the future. That happens either with new information provided in the present or with its destruction so that there is no witness in the present to tell what happened later to become part of someone's story.

For example, the moment you read these words will mark the time in the present that you are learning or reading this information, but that moment is not history until you are finished and it becomes the past spoken about in the future. So as these words are written, notice that our lives and stories are recorded in the present in the hope of being told in the future. But His-story, the history of the Creator, will forever be known for the rest of each one of our lives as long as it is known by someone and told correctly.

Know Your Story

Many have claimed they know their history, but they do not. Many have claimed His-story is man's history—the history of a corrupt and evil government—but as much as it makes sense, it is not true. We have even heard many people say, "Know your history," but they did not know that human beings do not have a history—we have stories and a testimony with the Creator. When we are born, our stories with Him begin. They are already planned out, but He leaves us in charge of deciding how each one will end. Regardless of how we choose, it is understood that the Creator gives us free will to allow us the opportunity to find our own purpose.

If you choose to live in the past, that is your choice. If you decide to live life having to choose between good and evil, that is totally up to you; just make sure you choose wisely! From birth to death, our stories create chapters in His-story, and they account for the time we have experienced on earth with Him as He oversees our moral obligations and commitments. No matter what we do in His world, it is His-story; He brings it into existence.

The Creator gave us our beginning, purpose, and direction and knew us before we could ever learn ourselves, for He gave us life. Whatever age we live to see, that's our journey with the Creator making His-story and our story. If a person lives to the age of sixty, that is the length of his or her story, and the time spent with the Creator makes that person a part of history and his or her time, with evidence of having been.

Our story also begins with our parents' stories, filled with their desires and disappointments. Children often follow in the footsteps of their parents, so parents' stories influence those of their children. Whatever the Creator saw our parents needed, asked for, or prayed to Him for, He granted it. So be careful what you wish for. Our parents—and no one else—are responsible for us up to a certain age. A child's beginning creates new chapters for them, and they are to guide and nurture that child. Until children reach an age of responsibility, their parents' job is to prepare them for the world, show them how to face challenges, equip them for any battles and adversity, help them find their gifts, talents, and purpose, and guide them so they can live out their dream and that purpose.

Our life starts with our parents' joined stories, but the choices we make determine the outcome. If we go through life without the proper guidance and without knowing our purpose, we will lose sight of our dream and destiny or get off our journey's path. A good place to start searching our parents' stories is their birth certificates. Check it for the race, and then chase it back. There is a history we need to know—the stories of our parents and where we begin in them. The only reason so many kids are lost and have behavior problems is that they are living out the wrong in their parents' story; the children are wearing shoes that do not fit, are bad, or are contaminated.

Many do not know the stories that include them—the true stories of their mother's and father's purpose and walk with the Creator and why the Creator brought them into existence. How can a poor child know his or her purpose if the child does not know the parents have one or even why the parents conceived him or her? Often missing is the story of the father, the one who most often leaves the home after placing life into the mother, who brings that child into existence. Other stories we need to know that include us are those in the Bible, starting from its beginning—the story of Adam and Eve, the story of Abraham and his two sons, and the story of Noah and his three. But it is imperative that you know the story of the Hebrew Israelites, the original children of Israel.

Your talent or gift is your moment in time that records the beginning and ending in your story with the Creator. If you have a wonderful singing voice, that is your talent given to you by the Creator. As long as you are able to sing, that defines your purpose, path, and journey, your history or relationship with Him. That journey is the story you made with and for the Creator as you live to use it to feed yourself and your family.

What you do or have done in your life is of your own decision, so make it a good one. "Make them remember you," as others have done in their lives. If Albert Einstein had not walked with the Creator and used his talents in math, science, and history to express his theory of relativity, $E = mc^2$, we would not know the Creator's work, this story, or His-story in Einstein as a scientist and mathematician. If Thomas Edison (and Lewis Latimer) had not walked with the Creator and recorded how a filament light bulb burns more slowly by carbonizing a piece of cotton thread, we would not know his talent, this history, or His-story. And if Sir Isaac Newton's journey with the Creator had not been recorded in documents, we would not know of his law of motion (explained in the equation $F=ma$) by using mathematics.

No matter what talent or gift you may have or what you have done or are doing with your life, His-story is the foundation of its existence. Our only assignment is to tell His-story, to tell others about our story with Him in it, and reap the benefit of advancement. Advancing is blessing, providing us with a better life of happiness. Every day we are here to set examples, teach what we know about the Creator from our experience, and nurture others who do not have the knowledge so we can save generations and preserve our many legacies. We are in His-story and time; we are historians who live to discover and count the days of God's existence with us and to tell others about His work while we are here.

History is the study of past events—knowledge acquired by investigation—but we must search to know what took place to tell it accurately and later live it. Many do not know their history, have not searched to understand the many events that have taken place, or do not realize the purpose of it. They do not know that their time, relation, walk, and journey are with the Creator. But man must be smart enough to search to find the answers, to control his life and his surroundings to gain mind over what matters. This information is important; whatever we learn from our walk is what we pass down to our children and our children's children, good or bad. Therefore, what we leave behind must be good, for our legacy is to make those who do not know us remember us. Each of our lives is His-story but just one small part of it, directed by the Creator.

Remember—God did not write, so He created or brought us forward to write for Him. He puts each of us on the path so we can tell His-story; this is His legacy, created through the stories of each one of us. So as we move on in life, understand, history is not about learning it just so we can blame others for wrongdoing; it's for us to learn who we are, our purpose, and what we can do. It is for us to seek what interests us so we can improve on it and then make changes. Make them remember you! Go get it and live your legacy now!

T W O

Language

Of all the subjects we were taught in school, language has always been one of the most enjoyable. The thrill was in learning the alphabet, sight words, and how to read and speak. Later we were told it is called communication, but how can it be when it is good only among the people who understand the language from that region? What happens when your language is used outside the community from which it originated? What is communication called then? How will you communicate with others who do not know your language, and what will you learn to apply in your life?

Communication

Communication is about exchanging information, knowledge, and news. It is about sending and receiving information. To communicate is to share. Sharing can mean enjoying something with others and having something in common with them. When we are communicating, we are sharing and exchanging information with the intent of understanding each other. And so we learned that language is a system of communication. It is the way we group sounds, represented by letters, to make words; combine words to make sentences; and articulate ideas to each other. We learned how to write essays, letters, reports, papers, and resumes with language. We also learned reading comprehension, parts of speech, and punctuation marks. We learned that language is the study of expression, speech, and writing. Schools have put a lot of focus on communication, but I always thought language had to be more. Thinking, all the way back to grade school, the furthest we went was taking a foreign language or studying abroad.

I turned to the Bible, which says, "In the Beginning was the Word, and the Word was with God, and the Word was God." In that sentence, *word* refers to language and God; the Creator is the Spirit, the communicator, and the only language. But that still was not enough! I spent months and years trying to understand its purpose. And then the question came to me, what else might God want us to know and do with language? I responded to myself, *God want us to understand and know about each other.* He wants us to know that language is about culture and our different experiences. It is about our identity—where we came from and what makes us who we are. Language is about our origin and the work people do to build up their land and how they make it last. Language is also about people building nations, cultures, and communities. Overall, language is about us.

Understanding Others

The nature of understanding others lies in knowing where they come from, what skills they possess, and what religious or spiritual beliefs shape their characters and personalities. You see, we are learning each other's identity. The way we pronounce our words and the manner in which we speak tell others about where we came from and what makes us who we are. When we speak to each other, our accents and dialects from our cultures, locations, and nations come out. In many cases, you can recognize a person's identity by the way he or she dresses. So not only are we communicating in speech, but we are also learning about each other visually.

Language is also about traditions and civilizations and the different races, not just about speaking or communicating. Communication is part of a language or a people, but it is not all there is to know. You see, communication just tells us something is being said, but identity tells us the characteristics of who is saying it and why. It is the experience of the many environments that is most important because we are learning from one another. We are learning how to appreciate one another and how to tell our stories based on where we came from. If someone came from somewhere around the world to visit our home, wouldn't we learn about their traditions and experiences as well? Communication is about an overall experience, not so much what a person says or sounds like alone.

Our Differences

Most of us may not understand a word a foreign person says, but we are quick to experience their food or customs without even knowing them. I know sometimes differences create problems, but we have to find out what we have in common and work out our differences while being reasonable and logical. Language is for us, and it belongs to us. It is about us learning and finding our uniquenesses, ideas, skills, and talents, and passing them down to other generations. It is about our legacy and most of all our cultures.

Language shows our differences and the various ways in which we communicate. It has been used to make friends and allies. We used art in trading, teaching, and fellowshipping, and many have used it to conquer territories. Those who create the best weapons gain the most power. Language has also been used to establish cultures, tribes, religious habits, and ethnic groups. People have taught each other their ways of life or cultural survival skills, such as farming, hunting, and fishing. They have displayed their inventions and unique creations, and they have even held wrestling and dancing competitions to show off their cultural talent. No matter how talented or gifted one is, the Creator made each one of us artistically unique for a reason. Differences create problems, and problems are to be solved. After all, if there were no differences among people, there would be no need to communicate.

With all the different types of people divided into many groups based on origin of land, language, dialect, religion, color, and other things, language is the only thing that explains how we became who we are. Schools taught us the basics—the alphabet, sentences, reading, and writing—and as you can see, they did not take it any further to teach us who we are. They left the teaching about nations and cultures up to the history teachers. If they had taught the history of people and language together or had made the connection between the two, more people would be living in the reality of their dream and know more about who they are. We would have learned what is expected of us. And so, as my memory became refreshed, I understood language and communication as the tools used to build nations and cultures.

Our Journey

As humans began to evolve, the Creator already had a language system in place for them to communicate with Him and others. The Creator, who was not of flesh, became man's conscience, his confidence, and most of all, his spirit to guide him along his journey in search of self. If you recall the tales of the first man, you know he did not speak a language. He went off and found land, built nations, started cultures, and became part of one. At the beginning of time, when there were no such things as words, early people made sounds, nothing we would today call words. Such noises were similar to the sounds animals—wolves, dogs, monkeys, and others—make. Today we think of those sounds as a form of communication. Other times, people used body movements such as hand motions to express ideas, somewhat similar to sign language. If you have ever traveled the world or spoken to someone who speaks a different language, you will understand how this unique form of communication has taken place. You actually witness a physical way of communicating nouns and verbs, the most important types of words in a language. You also experience their culture and unique way of life.

We have done great things and are capable of doing much more. Go get it! For ages, we have used drawing to express our thoughts. For example, if you have been to Egypt and seen inside one of the pyramids, you know they have just drawings on the walls, no recognizable words, called "hieroglyphs." Only a few people with skills and unique abilities were accepted to write. Those inscriptions contain expressions of secrecy, magic, and language, but only those who understood the translation knew their meaning and could use them. One important inscription placed outside one of the temples says "Know thyself," which is the key to life. Egyptians used a religious doctrine of discipline called the Mysteries, also known as "the first system of salvation," handed down in secrecy among the select few.

This system was developed for the purpose of writing, reading, and teaching. Note that it was known as the first system of salvation because it was the first religion, the first faith known of the Creator, and understood and taught only by Egyptian priests. Understand that it was God's people who taught all, and that everything the people learned was passed down through the generations but came from Him, the Creator. This is what you inherited. This was their education and the only knowledge passed down to generations for growth; it is the key to life.

All civilizations and many great minds, or what we believe are great minds, have studied in Egypt or taken knowledge from the Egyptians in some form. They include Socrates, Plato, Aristotle, Alexander the Great, and even Moses and Jesus, who studied under the Egyptian Mystery System. In the Bible, Moses turning a shaft into a snake and Jesus walking on water are examples of using magic expressions. But remember it all started in Egypt—a place, a nation, a culture of people.

Much later, we developed more sophisticated means of communication—telegrams, mail delivery companies, CB radio, and then telephones to formally reach out to each other and tell those stories. Today, we have advanced our modes of communication to cell phones, computers, and the internet, all of which are designed to let us make connections with one another around the world. But we cannot stop there. We must take our inheritance to the next level.

Almost seven thousand languages are spoken every day. Over seven billion people in the world speak at least one of them. Each of us has a story to tell through language. For thousands of years language has been our way of communicating, translating, and telling one another our stories, testimonies, and experiences. This is what makes us who we are and helps us know where we come from.

As you can see, the Creator brought language into existence for us to talk to and listen to each other, but most of all for us to learn about one another and Him. Everyone is here for a reason, so we have to be compassionate about life. We are the heirs of languages. We are the translators, narrators, and communicators of this world and the writers, speakers, and storytellers. Remember—the main reason that languages exist and that it is so important for us to learn how to speak, read, and write is so we can be better at telling others about our different experiences and journeys with Him. History and language go together. Language is His way for us to communicate with Him and one another. It is how we remember His-story and our journey with Him and keep it going and relevant. No other subjects matter without learning language first. It is the Creator's way that makes up our character, appearance, presentation, and first impressions by culture, ethnicity, and beliefs. These things express who we are on the outside and within. If people cannot at least read and write, everything else is meaningless. Why we did not learn where we come from and who we are first, I do not know. But all this should have been explained from the beginning, in grade school.

This is why I refer to language as the Creator's way of showing our differences, or the language of science. When you substitute the word *science* with its definition, "knowledge," language becomes the knowledge or the identity of the people and how they communicated, that is, the transferring of intelligence from one person to the next. Clearly, language is a gift and our way of communicating with each other and the Creator so we will not become lost, speechless, or disconnected from each other and from our purpose.

Language of the Arts

Language is where it all begins because it is also art, a product of human activity that expresses working skills, talents, or unique abilities. Before there were alphabets, early civilizations used those expressions to communicate and survive. Language is what makes all of us different and unique in our own right. No two people or groups were alike and expressed themselves in the same way. Art is work created only by human beings and, in most cases, made by their own hands, talents, and/or skills gained through practice, experience, or study. Even with visual art we made and created things such as paintings, sculptures, architecture, and ornamentation. Remember we were speaking way before we ever learned alphabets, words, and grammar.

Misuses of Language

Another form of language is performance art, which requires practice. Some examples are theater, film, dance, music, sports, literature, and fighting. These exist for entertainment, and they allow us to survive, take care of our families and ourselves, and make our way through life without begging and becoming a slave to or dependent on someone. Many of us have used our skills in these areas to create generations of wealth because there is always someone willing to pay others for their performance.

But there is another side to language or culture that not everyone is happy about, which has created new groups that aren't going in a good direction. Hollywood has changed over the last decades, and not everyone there is positive and morally driven. Hollywood in the twenty-first century has created some type of anti-God cult that is not good for our society or future generations. It has turned into more like an evil political party. The people in this industry will do almost anything for money and fame. Movies, television shows, magazines, and other performances and advertisements today seem to be obsessed with sex, violence, drugs, and gender identity disorder. Movie executives and directors use performing arts as a means by which to change our society, manipulate emotions, and destroy our children. They are using language not to communicate positive ideals but to tear us down. We can no longer give them a free pass in the name of acting. Real lives are affected by their work. These executives and directors get paid to manipulate desperate actors and innocent viewers. They create scenes in movies and on television with innocent and desperate actors being unfaithful to their real-life husbands or wives. In some cases, these actors end up fornicating with the other actors afterward.

Actors are being trained to lower their self-worth and are taking pride in selling themselves out for a fee and a yearly award. The manipulators create roles for these actors being raped on one hand, and on the other, show another actor performing the rape act. There are other scenes of straight men, women, and children acting as if they are homosexual, and some end up being that way after the filming. Why must every film or television show promote a community or a group of people that make up only 1 percent of the population? I do not know. What is wrong with promoting positive ideals in a show that displays growth, a traditional family, and legacy building? Acting in or viewing these negative scenes is not living your legacy; it is destroying it. I have seen other scenes in which an actor tears up the Bible. The Bible is a history book of many stories and legacies of our ancestors' journeys. It is the blueprint to life. Where does it say that to be successful you must disrespect the Creator of all?

The average viewers think what they see is acceptable and real. If the focus of these film executives, directors, and actors is to guide people away from God by showing sex, drugs, violence, and gender identity disorder in every film and taping, it shows the end is near. An actor who takes on these types of film roles is gambling with life. The same is true for parents who allow their children to play these characters. This miscommunication will leave us more divided. Division seeks power. Power needs controlling. How can there be any good in the world if we are not communicating properly and effectively? We have to put politics aside and learn how to be a nation, a culture, and a community again. If being against God and the ancestors' ideas is their only message, how can there be any good left in the world? It seems almost impossible for the average person to be in Hollywood for a long period and not turn against God; the odds are not on the actor's side. Just because it is called acting does not mean it is not affecting real people.

You can choose activities that make the world a better place or ones that degrade it. Choose wisely. And then work. No work, no success.

Comprehend Their Language

And so, we live in a world of language. With language comes letters and words, and when they are put into a particular order, they mean something. Language comes from one's environment, and every time we speak to each other, who we are and where we came from comes out. The words we speak give others some idea of the geographical location, nation, culture, or community we live in. For example, in America, people who sound their vowels hard have most likely lived up north, and if you hear others drag out their vowels, chances are they are from the south.

Words have a great influence on our lives, so we have to be careful what we say. They can make or break us; they can change our future in seconds. Certain words can build our confidence, and others can tear it down. That is why we must understand language and the differences in our nations, cultures, and communities: to better communicate and understand each other. We must learn how to comprehend what we say, read, see, and hear. Comprehension is one of the main reasons we are so divided, and it cannot be achieved without completely understanding language—both spoken and written. Anytime we take only a part of what someone else has said or written and then make it the single point of the whole story without considering everything, we have made a misjudgment; we have failed to fully understand the story. You would have to know and examine all that was said and how the extracted part was used in the sentence to understand what it means. The setting, tone, and word order must be taken into account before you can come to any conclusion. If you take selected words and put them in two different orders, in most cases the meanings will not be the same.

Comprehending the whole picture is very important in understanding other people and their writing. This is especially so for the words in the Bible. Many people read the Bible, but not everyone comprehends its lessons and applies them to their lives. It can be hard for some ministers, preachers, and priests to interpret the Bible correctly if they don't consider culture when examining it. Because many of us struggle with comprehension, real life issues can be a serious problem. Reading without full comprehension makes us just a reader, but reading with understanding gains us wisdom and knowledge. The failure to understand language and the whole picture in which the words appear can corrupt our thinking and leave us vulnerable to manipulators and oppressors.

THREE

Science

From the beginning of human existence, everything known to man has been called science, and all science comes from the Creator. Science is simply what things are, and also describes what makes them work. Nothing can work without humans showing and applying action. No animal has been able to achieve the things we have. They need us. The Creator gave the world to us. We are science's greatest work and discovery. Everything exists for us to learn and figure out, and those who do they are called scientists.

We Make Things Work

We are the heirs and descendants of science and scientists, and so we are scientists ourselves. From the moment of conception we have been scientists, exploring and figuring things out. A scientist typically takes his learning through a scientific process or methods by observation, forming a hypothesis, experimenting, and drawing a conclusion. Most people just need to be told they are scientists by nature and work is expected of them. As scientists, our job is to explore, work, and study all things brought into our existence. We study the beginning and ending of all those things of our interest, their purposes and functions. We study causes and effects and the reasons for them. And because everything is the effect of what caused it to exist (which is God), everything, including us, comes from the Creator and is science.

Taking It Further

In grade school, we were taught that biology is the scientific study of all living things, including how the different species might have evolved over millions of years. We were taught that chemistry is the study of matter, its various states, and how it changes. It involves the individual components things are made of, how they change when exposed to different environments, how they can be broken down, and how they can rebuild themselves. We were taught that physics is the study of matter (apart from chemistry), energy, forces, their interactions, and how they react under different conditions. We became aware that astronomy is the study of the planets and other stellar bodies, and how they interact with one another. Only those who were curious about the sciences were told they could be scientists; the rest of us did not know we already were one. What many of us did not learn about science, or what we put less focus on, is what science really means to us and how to apply it to our lives.

You see, we were taught science within the parameter of existence—what things are, how they look, and where they come from. We treated science as a thing that required only that we look, touch, and listen. As a result, many of us did just that and nothing afterward. No work, no progress. We learned that science is simply identifying things that exist—the "what" in the things we see, hear, taste, feel, and smell. If we had just approached science as a verb—as something to do, as something that engages us—we would have seen our purpose, and many of us would have done more with it. The Creator brought all things into existence for human beings to see how far we can go. Never did it occur to many people that to go far in life, one must first be willing and ready to act, become curious, and use imagination.

Merriam-Webster's online dictionary at merriam-webster.com defines *science* as "the state of knowing; knowledge as distinguished from ignorance or misunderstanding." Knowledge is information or data known and collected on anything on this planet or from any corner of this universe. But knowledge is more than that. It is not just the obtaining of information; it is also how far we can take that information—maybe to the next level of its created purpose for the use of something else. According to my observation, the word *knowledge* has two parts, *know* and *ledge*, or we can say *now* and *edge*, which mean exactly what they appear to mean. To know is to become aware. The part *now* means "at this moment in time." The words *ledge* and *edge* describe the end or the outside limit of something. All things beyond that are part of the unknown—the place where we have stopped thinking and pursuing. And that is where our imagination (which is, according to merriam-webster.com, "the creative ability to form images, ideas and sensation in the mind") needs to explore. But first, we must become curious enough to seek past what is beyond the unknown ledge or edge.

Becoming More Curious

A little curiosity is not enough. We must be curious enough to take what is unknown to a known state of existing. The place of the unknown is undiscovered, is not thought of, and has no name until we become curious and suspicious and allow our imagination to explore and give it a name to bring it to life. We have to look beyond what we know about everything. Knowledge is limited by what we have learned, but imagination will take us into uncharted territory—places we have never gone before. Imagination will keep us going, but the lack of exploring further limits our thinking. We can imagine all we want, but we won't get anywhere unless we take assertive action to find answers. If we aren't curious about ourselves, our own psyches, how can we gain the understanding needed to move to the next level in human life?

Explore More

The imagination within science prompts us to explore outside the perimeter of our teaching, and when we do not, our minds stop growing. Knowing is completely our responsibility. It requires that we continue to think and use our minds instead of accepting what someone else has told us are facts, without ever researching and thinking for ourselves. Until we take the little that we know to the very end of its original purpose, it is not knowledge; it is just awareness. Knowing includes imagining the possibilities, and with imagination, there can be no end. We cannot limit our thinking by wanting just to be aware of things when we can gain more by taking it to the end and beyond for a complete and accurate understanding.

Why do many science classrooms focus on teaching about plants, rocks, animals, planets, and everything else separately? Those topics are not what science means to human beings and their purpose; they do not connect to us. We spend too much time learning facts about everything without connecting those facts with ourselves. We have to educate ourselves about the truth about who we are as people and where we come from so we will no longer be misguided and led down the wrong path of destructive thinking that we do not matter and have no purpose. Knowing one's purpose determines one's direction and success. The path we take will be negative if we do not understand where we are going. Science is about human beings, and if you take away one, neither exists.

We are all born scientists, explorers, and practitioners. Our birth, existence, and purpose certify who we are. We do not need a certificate to validate who we are. We were put here on this earth to explore and practice, but we need guidance to perfect the skill. Science is for us, and we can identify it only by the use of our five senses, as well as the sixth one—thinking, or common sense. What we need most is to put our skills to work. No other species was given this much power. If you look around, you'll see that everything our senses come in contact with is of science, but it requires us to know and figure things out to take what we have learned to the next level.

What we see and hear in this current position is real and important but only to those who can witness, articulate, experience, and change it. Every encounter or experience we engage in is for us and by us through our senses. What we learn, discover, or uncover is what is expected of us, for us to do and apply. Our two most important senses are sight and hearing because whatever we see or hear could be an illusion. We do not want to be a part of anyone's magic trick, because others will witness what we did when we were here. Science is simply the knowing of all things and their purposes. So if the reason for living and the cause and effect are not taught, many of us will never know our true purpose or what exists within us that makes us who we are.

I asked the obvious: how can anything hold us back when we are supposed to be here and go further? When I put everything aside to just think, I came to one conclusion. If those who struggled with life could have learned science using imagination and curiosity, they would have known what to do and how to apply science to solve their problems. They would have seen where they fit into the problem and then made adjustments. We can solve our own problems, but we have to put in the work so we'll never have to deal with them again. Everything must be taken through a process, the scientific method:

1. Make an observation.
2. Ask a question.
3. State a hypothesis.
4. Conduct an experiment.
5. Analyze the results.
6. Draw a conclusion.

This new knowledge would have built their confidence, and today, they would have known that their life mattered and they weren't here by accident. If science is everything and everything that exists has a reason and a purpose for its existence, then we too are science and possess the same characteristics. But first, we must understand that science comes from the Creator, which should be taught from the beginning. We are from the imagination of the Creator, and we are one. The world belongs to us so make them remember you. We are the only reason both exist. And without us, there would be no one to say they exist or don't exist.

Nevertheless, many people will tell you that science and the Creator are two different things and not connected in any way, just to keep you from finding the truth about who you are. If this were so, that would mean taking existence and knowledge out of science, leaving nothing. Clearly that cannot work. If science consists of all things that exist, knowledge is information about all those things, and God is the Creator of all, then nothing—living or nonliving—would exist without a beginning or a cause. There cannot be one without the other, because they both come from the same source—the Creator and human beings' reality. In other words, science is just another way human beings describe the work of God, the Creator.

Existence: We Have Always Existed

There are people who will make you believe you do not have a purpose just so you can live in fear, doing nothing. They want you to live in fear, not thinking, expecting death too soon, and never trying to advance yourself. Many of those same people want you to believe that life stops after you are dead by teaching you there are nonliving things. But if you evaluate nonliving things with the Most High's science, you realize all things exist. If anything can be seen, heard, felt, tasted, smelled, spoken about, or thought of, then it is living and living for a reason—even you. As long as something has energy, an ability, a name that can be spoken, or a location, it is living and not dead. Our existence or presence makes all things exist to us.

Everything that is living also grows and has life but only in an individual's reality. Our reality, experiences, and observations of things are alive because they are in our present state of being, which makes them real to us. And as long as we exist, all things exist, and the Creator God exists and is not dead. For example, the Most High continues to live on within us. Whether you are Christian, Jewish, Buddhist, Hindu, Muslim, or an atheist, He exists as long as we at least say His name. Our not knowing the purpose or science of who we are has made many people generate negative energy, and as a result, many are destroying their lives and creating hate. Many are not contributing, investing, and inventing in their homeland. They think they are already dead, so keep your head up and start thinking. You are not dead. Make them remember you. Some of you might not be functioning because you're being misguided, but do not give up. Just keep living!

When people pass away and are cremated, they are not dead and do not completely go away. Their remains become ashes and change to a different form. The same thing happens with other objects. They take on a new purpose. In life, we have to change as well. Ashes, rocks, dust, bricks, roads, and buildings are living and growing. As they become old, they break down or appear cracked, like many of us. Metal can become rusted, melted down, remade, or reprocessed, but it does not go away; it keeps growing and living. It may not live long in its original form, but it is still living and can grow. Our waste never dies. After it has been processed through the sewage system, oftentimes it is disposed of or burned. Some animal waste is aged and then packaged for sale as fertilizer. A chair in the room, the clothes we wear, and the cars we ride in are living because of our senses.

Matter, which is in a state of gas, liquid, solid, or plasma, can change into another of those states through the use of energy. This ability to be transformed helps to keep all things alive, not limiting them to moving or being in transition. This is the type of physical energy we need to have when we are feeling down and thinking we cannot get up and go any farther. Energy can be in the form of either potential (stored) or kinetic (in motion) and can change form. It is in our senses, each word we speak. When we touch, smell, taste, hear, or see things, we make them come alive. Each word spoken, a simple touch, a loud sound, a sour taste, or the sight of a family member not seen in a while makes it living. Even when an animal is killed for food, it is not dead; its body is alive with proteins and nutrients for a tasty meal. When fruits and vegetables are disconnected from branches or roots, they are not dead; they are alive with plenty of vitamins and minerals that help us stay healthy. As long as something is spoken of, thought of, discovered, uncovered, contracted, transferred, or generated, it is not dead. There is nothing dead about you.

In the Beginning

Those same scientists and educators would have you believe that the universe began only after the big bang, as though the universe created or formed itself and there is no God. But if that is so, what happened before the big bang? There had to be something that existed before the big bang that caused it to explode. In this case, that could have been the Creator. He existed and knew that there was going to be a big bang long before it formed the universe and all that it brought before us. If you catch a ball thrown to you, someone or something must have sent it your way. So it is with the theory of the big bang. For it to explode, someone or something must have first caused it to exist. That is what many scientists refuse to bring to our attention. They do not mention the need for God's existence before the big bang could have happened. The big bang theory is just that: a theory. Although it is accepted as "truth" in the scientific community, there is no way to really know what caused the creation of the universe.

Remember that in the beginning of the Bible, God said, "Let there be light," and there was light. Well, that light could have been the big bang. Right after that, God separated light from darkness. How do we get light now? Light comes from the sun and the stars. That means we got the light from the sun and anything else only after the big bang. This theory tells us that God created long before there was a universe, earth, and the first man. God has always been here; He never left. We are here for one reason only, and that is because God wanted us to be here, and He gave us life.

However, purpose of our lives explains the purpose of science. As science tells us, there is a cause and effect for everything that happens. The same goes for us: we came from someplace, and we are here for a reason. This is why I refer to science as existence; it is the Creator's work. For something to exist, there must be a cause and it must have an effect, or purpose. God brought forth all things for a purpose and then left man in charge and responsible for finding the many answers and figuring out what to do with them. We are the true guides to our destinies. God gave us free will. We can choose to perceive what happens as negative or positive. It's up to us. If we understand we have the power to control, or to at least influence, how we respond to the good and bad in the world, then we can exercise our free will to make life happier and more prosperous. In short, we can take responsibility, whereas we did not when we believed we were leaves scattered in a cold autumn wind.

Creationism: What Causes Us

A main source of confusion for us is that we were taught that we were created but were never told we were brought into existence by some cause. On the other hand, common sense clearly tells us that no one creates life. Creating comes from using hands, and the closest thing to creating life is cloning. To date, no human has been cloned, at least that we know of. Some doctors save lives, but those lives already exist, so they are not being created. Plastic surgeons can change the appearance of human beings, but they do not create life. As we all know, doctors are not God and do not physically bring life together, although they may try to practice as though they do.

As merriam-webster.com says, "Energy is neither created nor destroyed." And the Bible tells us the Most High created Adam and Eve. For us, He caused or did something with atoms, other matter, and energy to bring us into existence. Atoms, made up of protons, neutrons, and electrons, are the basic units of matter. Matter is anything with mass and can be in the visible form of solid, liquid, gas, or plasma. (There are other forms, such as Bose-Einstein condensate, in extreme conditions, but they are outside our more simplified discussion here.) When combined into elements, atoms form matter—what we see and what we are. Energy can be either potential (stored and available for use) or kinetic (motion, which is seen when something is moving). Energy is the force or power generated by the charge of atoms, which gives any matter the ability to work.

How can we be created or destroyed if we are made from energy and all these things? There is no creating in this process. There is just the cause and effect of transferring, the charging of energy, and the reaction of many chemicals.

Therefore, the Most High did not just create us. He also caused us to exist. The only thing that might have been created is what came first in the beginning of time, not what came after that reacted to it, for that is the effect. Remember—the big bang caused life or the absolute beginning of it, and everything that came afterward is the effect. Cause is the reason an act or a condition happens just so we can have the effect. Effect is produced by cause, and as we know, everything happens for a reason or a cause. For example, the Most High caused the beginning so we can have a present and a future and caused hydrogen and oxygen atoms so we can have air, clouds, rain, and then water. Understand that Adam and Eve are the cause of families, generations, and everyone who has existed since then, including us and those who will come after us. This is another reason why He gave man and everything around him a purpose. We are the effects of Adam and Eve, which make them the cause or the reason for our existence. As for any of your ancestors, with struggle or not, you are the effect and the beneficiary of their legacy.

No Evidence

The fact of the matter is that no evidence or experiment demonstrates that we were actually created, but plenty shows how we came into existence by the science of the Creator. All of us know from experience that we were made by our mother and father and came into life at birth. However, human life does not exist until you have breath in the body, functional organs, and body parts. Neither the doctor nor our mother and father used their hands to place any body parts or organs in us or created us during birth. For a large amount of time, we lived in our biological father before being transferred to live in the womb of our mother and then brought into the world. When we became an adult and found our own companion of the opposite sex, we repeated the process of generating another generation, which will then bring forth other ones. This process never stops because God intentionally brought life into existence for the purpose of generating and powering the idea of growth. Other evidence is in birth defects. It takes an unbalanced system, the wrong atomic number in an element, or the abuse of some substance by one or both parents for a birth defect to occur. It does not come from the hands of the Creator, for it is written that He is of everything that is good.

Gravity, oxygen, and hydrogen are some of the things that allow human beings to live on earth. Organs, bones, flesh, the eleven systems of the body, and other factors make our bodies work. They cause people to live, and people are their effects. As you see, leaving this information out of teaching means individuals will not be able to see how unique and spectacular they are. Instead, they will think they don't matter to life and or have a purpose.

The Afterlife

There is life after death, and many people cannot wait to die because they have given up on earth. Others claim to seek the afterlife because they are curious and think they might be missing something. Many religious people believe in reincarnation, the concept that a new life starts in a different physical body or form after a biological death, but that is just one theory. Many Christians seek the afterlife in hopes of meeting their maker and being in heaven. Others seek the afterlife hoping to be with their loved ones who have already passed away. Some men of the Islamic faith also seek the afterlife to be with their god and/or to receive the expected reward of seventy-two virgins. We assume those who have passed away sought and prepared themselves for the next life.

Who is to say there is no life after death? Unless the unbelievers have the ability to leave this life and then return to tell the story of that experience, no one can prove there is no life after death. But we have heard of those who have gone through near-death experiences and claimed there is such a life. In one scenario, a person flatlines on the operating table and experiences a white light, or the feeling that they are levitating above the table as the doctor saves them. Although they've said these things happened, there is still no way of actually knowing.

We know only about the life we are in. Many of us find it hard to believe and accept anything other than what we know exists in our reality. But people would eventually believe there is life after death once they understood life before birth—the time before a human's life when two living beings of the opposite sex come together to produce another. Time is the only evidence we have that there is life after death because it keeps recording human life as time moves forward.

Technology has given us the ability to see the before-life through x-rays, ultrasounds, and other techniques. Still, no one truly knows his or her life as a sperm, an egg, an embryo, or a fetus. But we do know they all seek the next life or the next phase of life. A human sperm seeks the egg of a woman, they both seek the next life of an embryo for eleven weeks, and afterward a fetus seeks life outside the womb as a human being, about which it knows nothing until its birth into this world.

Even if we take the definition of *death*, it explains life only as it appears to human beings. Understand that only human beings can identify death as just that. The word *death* is just a group of letters put together by human beings to better label what they see at a certain part of life in our reality. "Death" defines only the end of life of human beings who move on to another life form on their journeys. Human life begins when the fetus stage is transformed into what we call birth, when breath enters the body, and it ends, by our definition, when the breathing stops. Death does not address life before or after those points.

The life of the sperm, the eggs, an embryo, and a fetus are not from this life because life has not typically started. Death does not exist at that stage because life has not yet taken place. You would have to be in the before-life to know God's interpretation, creation, and communication with that life form; no one truly knows that. In other words, there is no death in fertilization, conception, and on up to birth in humans. Death does not exist there because it was written here by humans for labeling life. Death happens only to humans. To know the truth takes the sperm, egg, embryo, and fetus to tell us what that life is truly like. The sperm, egg, and embryo cannot be put to death, and neither can human beings, because they all have energy, which cannot be created or destroyed. As long as they have tissues, chromosomes, DNA, and all else that allows human beings to move on to the next life and for science to do more with the remains, they are not dead and have not died.

As for life after being human, who can say the elder transformers are not looking down on us, watching to see what we are doing, or have not left us with the knowledge to uncover and discover because they know it matters?

If we'd been taught that science is nothing more than a form of discipline understood in three parts—natural, social, and formal—having good values would have been easy to obtain. Natural science teaches us how and why God created us. Social science teaches us about the behavior of God's greatest creation: man. Formal science teaches us about mathematics, computers, and technology and what human beings can do with the knowledge about the Creator and His purpose. If people knew themselves and their capabilities, they would never need to depend on other people to help them or their families. A famous Chinese proverb says, "Give a man a fish, and you feed him for a day. Teach a man to fish, and you feed him for a lifetime." People have to believe in themselves, and their talented hands can take them around the world with no limitation. They must see the world and their lives wherever they are as greatness. Greatness is in application; it comes from applying knowledge in everyday life so we will know and learn our true purpose. The Creator has given us everything, and all things that exist were created and brought forward for us and in His name.

Our Purpose

From the stories of our ancestors to the place and purpose of our birth, we have existed for a reason, and it should have been explained from the beginning of each one of our lives as that. What we do with our lives and how we carry ourselves today will be the information or science of we leave behind for others to learn about us. So it is important that we leave good lives about which to tell.

Not knowing one's self or the science of self creates chaos in one's life. The science of self means knowing who you are and what to do with that knowledge. To know yourself is to know your ability and God's plan for you. You take that knowledge and start implementing it in everything you do. You know what He wants from you, so do that and stay firm. Where no knowledge is gained or the received knowledge is corrupted, nothing positive will be established, and success will have no place to grow. Life at that point will become a waste, and you will have lived without a purpose and knowing what that purpose is. All things are here for us and are to be used and enhanced by us; there can be no science if we are not here and able to recognize and understand it. If we take the same approach with life and study the science of our individual self, we will understand life's importance and know our true purpose on earth. This process creates a legacy for our children to build upon and be proud of.

Science enables us to think and become curious. It prompts us to ask questions and to use our imagination to know and see just what we are dealing with if we decide to make any changes. Our purpose is to grow, and part of growing is making changes so we can better understand what we can do and become. We are the only species that knows what science is, and the only ones who can explore and study to improve it. One of the main purposes of science is for people to learn who they are and the unlimited things they can do and become. Once we understand why things exist, we will be better positioned to discover our purpose. Self-awareness, faith, and a positive outlook that cancels negativity will allow us to achieve our greatest potential. Searching and exploring are what the Creator intended for us to do. Because we too are the effects of the Creator, each of us is assured that we have a cause, a reason, and a purpose for existing.

The moral to this lesson is that we have to be willing to step into unknown territories that are outside our normal activities just to get ahead. We have to become scientists and start exploring life outside the territory we know. Instead of complaining about certain people having wealth, research what they did to get where they are and try it yourself. It does not matter if the person invested in buying homes or in the stock market; go learn what it takes to become successful too. If you've never had a business before, start one so you will know just what businesspeople have done, the risks they have taken, how they were able to hire employees and provide them with benefits, and more. We cannot be afraid to try something new. We need the courage to step out of our comfort zones. I know change can be terrifying to some of us sometimes. Just know that if there is anything keeping us back, it is our fear of the unknown. Change is the epitome of the unknown. The knowledge is already in you, so turn the negative into positive and go live out your legacy.

FOUR

Mathematics

For years, we have learned that math is the science of numbers—the study of time, quantities, shapes, and space. We learned arithmetic—how to put numbers in order and use them in adding, subtracting, multiplying, and dividing. After mastering the basics of arithmetic, most of us learned one or more of the advanced branches of mathematics: algebra, geometry, trigonometry, and calculus. Because not everyone's brain develops at the same time, we do not learn on the same level. So in school, we were divided into different groups based on our learning abilities. Little did we know that math was much more than using numbers. Thinking on this and my experiences, researching, and using common sense, I realized what math actually means, what its purpose is, and what the Creator might hope we learn by bringing math into our existence. This is what I discovered. Mathematics is simply about human beings making connections and building relationships with each other through life experiences. Math is about humans bringing things together and taking them away. And to do that, we must think critically and use common sense to solve problems and understand them.

Problem Solvers

Every great mind of the past, such as Galileo Galilei, Friedrich Gauss, Isaac Newton, Albert Einstein, Ethelbert Chukwu, Charles Bell, and David Blackwell, discovered something or some type of theory using numbers. But they were not in search of numbers. Instead, they had questions or problems they wanted to solve, and they used numbers to figure them out. They were searching to understand connections and relationships and what makes things work. Each of them was working on and solving life problems, not actual number problems. Note that each of them was using math word problems that were based in real life, and that's how problems were solved. All of us are mathematically born problem solvers; we are the heirs and descendants of mathematicians, and if we are solving problems, we too are mathematicians.

Just as the Creator gave us problems, He gave us answers, but we have to explore, act, connect, and build relationships to figure them out. Math is the blueprint for learning life's lessons, but no success comes without effort. Solving problems is part of life, and doing work, including using math, is how it is done and is required of us. Math is the means to solving and understanding problems and the mysteries of science. It doesn't matter what exists; math is how we solve problems, how we get things done, and how we bring things together or take them away.

Applying Effort

Understand that math is about human beings. Before numbers existed, we used math to make connections and build relationships without knowing we were using math. Math is for us, so it belongs to us. To what other species math is useful? You see, math is the verb of numbers; it tells us to do something and to do it with numbers. And so every time math has ever been presented to us, it has required us to do just that. When we apply something, we are in the act of doing that which makes math an application. Math is an application, defined at merriam-webster.com as "the act of putting something into operation," or simply applying effort. Math is a part of our lives but must be learned in the form of English.

Connecting Relationships

Math connects things to build new relationships, but it requires us to find ways to do it. From the beginning—the start of Adam and Eve and all our lives from that point forward—was mathematics. Adam and Eve are the ones who were brought together, and we are the outcome that continues to connect and build generations through actions. Math relates things to each other and gives them a purpose. Those relationships are the foundation of mathematics—adding, subtracting, multiplying, and dividing. These four foundations tell us what type of relationship to expect, and it gives us an outcome of how we define that relationship.

When we join things, they become a pair, molecule, group, team, substance, or some other new entity, which grows or sometimes separates. Once joined, they are in a new relationship. This also happens, for example, with mixing colors. Every time we mix two or more colors, they create a new color. The same is true with people. A man connects with a woman, and in their growing connection and relationship with each other, they become as one in a marriage. During the process of reproduction, we are added by birth, subtracted by death, and multiplied and divided when creating family for many generations to come.

Bring Things Together

Absolutely nothing that exists can connect or build a relationship unless it shows action or puts work into an operation. Work is what the Creator expects us do! Look around you. Everything connects and builds relationships. Math is everywhere, but we are not seeing it or doing the work to make it come to life. Word problems are the best example of applying math lessons to life. In school, we spent too little time learning how to solve number word problems. And because our teaching focused less on word problems and on math with so many different divisions and separations, we became confused about how to apply change in our lives. We never made the right connections to see how everything relates and comes together in real life.

Many of us do not understand math—what it is, its purpose, and how to grow—because many of us failed to connect with people, especially those who do not look like ourselves. The key to life is growth, and as we know, everything must grow. We are only holding ourselves back if we refuse to connect, build relationships, or associate with everyone. Who knows, the people you meet today may be able to connect you to someone who can change your life. If you never connect with positive people, you may never build a relationship of value. So just think: if you introduced me to a friend to help me buy a house, wouldn't that be the same as networking?

We connect and come together in all forms anyway, even in sports, so why can't we connect in the rest of life? If you connect the players, or bring them together as one, they are grouped as a team or a franchise. In every game, math controls and connects us to the time from start to finish via a timekeeper, stopwatch, or scoreboard. In the sport of boxing, every type of punch has its own connection, relationship, and number. The jab is one, the cross is two, the left hook is three, the right hook is four, the left body hook is five, and so on. In baseball, the bases are numbered first, second, third (and home). In football, the entire field is covered with numbers every ten yards, designating the distance from one end to the goalpost, and what players do during the game generates statistics. Plus, every game is played on a field or court of a specific dimension.

Just as when water is added to a plant (combined), when two or more things are joined, they will grow. Mathematics is the only activity that we were given by the Creator to help us do just that. We are supposed to grow, to be together, and to combine things. The Creator knew all this. He knew that many of us would go through difficult times and struggle, but we have to understand that math creates and changes circumstances. This is the main reason He left humans in charge of everything. He knows we are the only species that can bring things together or take them away. And so we are all connected and are related in some way, just as all colors are related to each other and all numbers are related to each other. Our chromosomes, DNA, saliva, fluid specimens, color, family, communities, and so on bring us all together. Even if we were trying to solve the most difficult of life's problems, such as poverty, math is what we would use. And so I honestly think that with the right math curriculum in schools and colleges, we would.

So you see, over the years, we were taught numbers, rather than math understanding, and we were told that math is the science of numbers because it exists. We treated math as science, what something is, knowing it has its own identity. If you study math outside of science, you will begin to see it in a different way. However, if science is everything that exists, math can be concerned only with how those things work, were made, and came into existence, and their purpose. If math were science, there would be no reason to call it "math," so it must mean something different from "science" and have its own purpose. Math and science are separate but should be taught together. What we have missed or overlooked through years of learning math is what it does and how to apply its purpose in our everyday lives. Math tells us to do something. Because math makes connections, builds relationships, and organizes them, it creates order and balance for growth. Its purpose is to bring things together that work, take them away when they do not, and then put them in order, ready to use.

Practicing

Lessons consist of knowledge practiced and rehearsed before we use them to move forward in life. Our lives need balance to assure proper function. So when we take these lessons, understand that we are practicing and exploring before we are tested. We cannot sit idly, thinking things will get better or something will knock on the door; we have to try extending ourselves, just to see what links, and build from that. We are not supposed to struggle; that idea is in our minds. People struggle mostly because they do not know what to do or are afraid of trying. The concept of gaining wisdom, knowledge, and understanding is implied here. To enrich our lives, we have to take knowing our problems and combine that with why they exist to understand the wisdom behind why they are affecting us. Once we understand the lesson, it is easy to apply it or do the work required to get it done. The world belongs to us, but we have to *Go Get It and Live Our Legacy Now* before it is too late.

How It's Done

No matter what subject in mathematics you choose, it deals with connections and relations. Why it is not taught this way, I do not know. Math also calculates as we do. According to merriam-webster.com, calculations are "a process that transforms one or more inputs into one or more results with a variable change." The key words here are *input* and *change*. You cannot receive either without work; you need to apply, act, and explore. Some people fail because they don't put forth any effort and just don't want to work. They are taking something away from themselves.

Math is part of us; it is simply how we do things. The better we understand how things are done, how they exist, and what their functions are, the better we will see what we can do and accomplish. Math commands us to act, research, and investigate. Its purpose is to help us find the connections and relationships—networking—between all things that exist in our reality to solve problems, especially the problems that divide us in hateful ways. Math exists for us to better understand those things, and we have to be willing to work to get results. Everything we do is math in some form, and whether we are working on a job, driving a car, getting an education, or something else, we're required to do things so we can succeed in becoming more connected and getting things done.

We are no different from numbers. If you do not believe me, think about the following examples.

Choose two numbers. Now combine them. No matter which ones you choose, their combination gives an answer—another number—and a relationship exists between them. Now remember numbers will not do anything until we connect them, apply a mathematical operation, or do the work. In a numerical sequence, a number comes before and after every number except zero. There is no number before it. That area before the zero is called the unknown, the place where it was conceived. However, it is impossible to get to the next number until you go through one that connects them all. You can add, subtract, multiply, or divide them, and each time, you will get a new relationship, an answer, a solution, a number, an outcome. For example, take the numbers six and four. Their relationship, connection, combination, and sequence are in 2, 10, 24 (and others): 6 − 4 = 2, 6 + 4 = 10, and 6 × 4 = 24. However, these same numbers also have a relationship with other family numbers. For example, 3 + 7 also equals 10. These connections keep building generations on to infinity. No matter what number you add, multiply, subtract, or divide with another number or object, there will be an answer, relationship, connection, solved problem, or new generation of numbers.

Example 4.1

Consider the ten numerals that make up all numbers: 0, 1, 2, 3, 4, 5, 6, 7, 8, 9. Those ten numerals connect all numbers to each other. All through infinity, those ten numerals keep doing work by repeating themselves: 0, 1, 2, 3, 4, 5, 6, 7, 8, 9, 10, 11, 12, 13, 14, 15, 16, 17, 18, 19, 20, 21, and so on.

Example 4.2

Another way to see the work of math or the connection is through related families of numbers in the basic multiplication tables. The 2s are half the 4s, 3s are half the 6s, 4s are half the 8s, 5s are half the 10s, and 6s are half the 12s. However, the first of each pair (2, 3, 4, 5, 6) is typically all you need to remember. To learn the first group is to learn the second at the same time. You can also find other times tables within the two groups. The 2s, in addition to the 4s, have a connection and a relationship with the 8s. The 3s connect and build relationship with the 9s and, in addition to the 6s, with the 12s. This concept is also the way to teach multiplication to young people in less time.

Example 4.3

Another unique way to see the connections and relationships is to look at the numbers after a number with a zero in the ones position in every table. If you follow the zero after it appears in the ones place, the base number keeps repeating itself.

2s: 2, 4, 6, 8, 10, 12, 14, 16, 18, 20, 22, 24, 26, 28, 30 ...
3s: 3, 6, 9, 12, 15, 18, 21, 24, 27, 30, 33, 36, 39, 42, 45 ...
4s: 4, 8, 12, 16, 20, 24, 28, 32, 36, 40, 44, 48, 52, 56 ...
5s: 5, 10, 15, 20, 25, 30, 35, 40, 45, 50, 55, 60, 65, 70 ...
6s: 6, 12, 18, 24, 30, 36, 42, 48, 54, 60, 66, 72, 78, 84 ...

Do you see it? Here is the set for the 7s placed on two lines so you can more easily see the repetition in the ones column:

7, 14, 21, 28, 35, 42, 49, 56, 63, 70,
77, 84, 91, 98, 105, 112 ...

In addition to the above relationship, the 9s table has many interesting relationships, especially in the numbers through 9×10. Look carefully below. Do you see it?

9, 18, 27, 36, 45, 54, 63, 72, 81, 90

To help you see, I will make a slight adjustment in that sequence (the numbers remain the same):

09, 18, 27, 36, 45, 54, 63, 72, 81, 90

Look more closely after the number 45. It keeps working. After it, the numerals are the reverse of the ones before—45 and 54, 36 and 63, and so on. Another important fact about the number nine is birth, for it is the symbol of life. It takes a mother nine months to nurture the greatest gift to life.

Example 4.4

Even the numeral zero has a relationship and makes a connection with numbers. You might think zero has no connection to other numbers since it means "none." But zero is important as a placeholder in numbers. For instance, we could not have the number thirty without a zero; we need zero to show that there are no ones with the three tens. So zero does have a value and an application for learning.

I once had a conversation with a woman whose four-year-old son could not grasp adding with the number zero. She said he did not understand why any number plus zero equals the other number, so I gave her some pointers on how to plant a seed in his mind. I told her to show him how zero appears in his surroundings. Take him to the car and show him the zero on the gas gauge. Tell him that when the dial gets to zero, the car no longer has gas (i.e., zero gas). Explain that if Mom does not go to work, she gets zero dollars. I also told her to get the egg carton out the refrigerator and show him what the carton looks like with zero, or no, eggs in it. Then go back and show him how to add with zero.

The point here is we have to get children to think and use their imagination to apply lessons to life. This is why I refer to math as the Creator's way of connecting and establishing relationships between all things. And if I replace the word *science* with its meaning, "knowledge," there is a connection to those things that exist. Math is the connection and the relationship to science. It is the how that explains the existence and the connection of all things at any given moment as they come in contact with each other.

Example 4.5

The most-often-used numbers are 1, 2, 5, 10, 20, 25, 50, and 100, and most of them represent a US currency.

Other important numbers are 9, 12, 15, and 25, all four of which affect our everyday lives.

- The number 9 connects us to or represents childbirth. It is the number of months it takes for a baby to fully develop in its mother's womb.

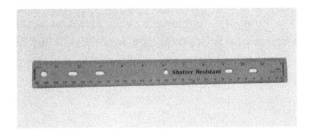

- The number 12 connects us to or represents the months of the year, is the number of inches in one foot (used in measuring many items in the United States), and divides our days into hours.

- The number 15 also connects us to or represents time, the most important moment in the life of man and woman that cannot be stopped. It represents the number of minutes in one quarter of an hour that we are here on earth. It is very important not to waste any of them.

- The number 25 connects us to or represents an accomplished stage in life. As a percentage, it is equal to one-fourth. It also connects us to the numbers 50 and 100, which represent other important stages.

Example 4.6

The number 100 is one of the most commonly used numbers. Almost everything we do in life is connected with this number. Percentages, fractions, estimations, and decimals are connected to 100.

Many of us were taught that reaching 100 is an accomplishment, something to aspire to. We were also taught, on the other hand, that life expectancy reaches 100. One hundred is the average number of years a population or a certain segment of the population can expect to live. Reaching 100 is statistically unusual. In our society, when a person reaches 100 years of age, he or she is considered blessed.

If the number 100 had been taught correctly in school, percentages would be much simpler to understand when calculating, estimating, rounding numbers, and making purchases. As a percent, 100 represents the total, the whole, all of something. So 100 by itself (not part of a percentage) sometimes symbolizes the whole of something or completion.

In measurement, 100 is the base for percentages, which are just a different way of expressing fractions. For instance, 25 percent of something is the same as one-fourth of it, because 25 percent = .25 = 25 divided by 100, which is 1/4. Similarly, 50 percent is the same as one-half, and 75 percent is the same as three-fourths.

This is the link showing how we apply numbers to real-life situations. Let us say I want to make a purchase and need to figure out a percentage of its price. I want to do it in my mind without pen or paper. The item's original price is $30.00, and it is being offered at 25 percent off. I can figure this several ways:

1. Since 25 percent is the same as one-fourth, it is being offered at one-fourth off the original price. One-fourth of $30.00 is simply 30 divided by 4, which is 7 1/2—or, in dollars, $7.50. So I will save $7.50 (and pay $30.00 − $7.50 = $22.50).

2. Or I can break 25 percent into parts that are easy numbers to work with in my head: 25 percent = 10 percent + 10 percent + 5 percent. I easily figure 10 percent of $30.00, which is $3.00. I know 5 percent is half of 10 percent, so 5 percent of $30.00 is half of $3.00, or $1.50. Now I add up the three parts for 10 percent + 10 percent + 5 percent, which is $3.00 + $3.00 + $1.50, or $7.50 off $30.00.

You can see, throughout the process of solving the problem, that I made many relationships and connections just to find the right combinations and sequences.

Math of Self

In Greek, math is commonly understood as "knowledge, change, and structure." As we have learned, knowledge consists of information, facts, and skills that a person acquires through investigation, experience, and education. But we cannot learn any knowledge without first exploring and then applying lessons to life. Math, the science of numbers, is the key that unlocks the mysteries of science. Math also gives order through sequences, combinations, and balance, opening the door to science. Since anyone can walk through an open door, science is available to all.

The mathematical balance in you and your life keeps your life from coming apart, becoming uneven, or causing problems for you. In other words, your life must be in order and balanced for you to function correctly. Order determines what should come first, second, third, and so forth in our lives, and keeps us balanced. Just as we plan and follow steps, laws, and rules, we use order to keep everything in our lives balanced, which gives us the best outcome.

If you understand order, you know that every connection is part of a system of order that tells us how it operates or works. A system is made up of a group of parts that come together in mathematical order to work together to perform a task. Order is the foundation for how a system works; it creates structure and allows the system to bring the pieces together. We are like a system, so the same thing happens with us—order allows us to function properly. Without the proper understanding of math, we would become unbalanced, or our actions would become dysfunctional. Our bodies would not be able to work properly, to play sports or perform academically.

We have to understand correctly why the Creator brought math into our existence. Take, for instance, the simple act of catching a ball. A system of several pieces is in place and designed for you to catch it successfully. In very simple terms, the first piece, or stage, of catching is to see the ball. The next is to use your hand. Most people have been taught that the hands come first, but you can't catch a ball unless you see it coming to you.

The idea is to understand that although there will be many rules and laws to follow, they are nothing more than a combination—sequences of numbers put in place to help us function, find balance, and make connections with life, the Creator, and each other.

Change is another part of math; it is the idea of making or becoming something different. In structure, math is the basis of an object and how it appears to one's observation or reality. With structure, all things have a scientific shape and size, and in every shape, you will always have a connection.

Another example is a person running for a political office. People who want to hold elected positions do not run for office unless they have a connection, experience, or talent in the field. No one should attend school if he or she does not wish to make a connection to learning and the teachers providing the lessons. Robbers do not rob banks or homes unless they have made some type of connection with robbery. Violence seeks and connects to violence. It has a shared interest in what is there or has been visited to know what perpetrators can connect with or take. However, crime would not exist if love were in the hearts of those who commit criminal acts. Violence removes all love connections. Through it all, love is the greatest solution and connector, for it brings all of us together in a positive way. If all of us acted out each day in love, there would be no room to hate. During his 1964 Nobel Peace Prize lecture, Dr. Martin Luther King Jr. put it this way:

> Violence never brings permanent peace. It solves no social problem; it merely creates new and more complicated ones. Violence is impractical because it is a descending spiral ending in destruction for all. It is immoral because it seeks to humiliate the opponent rather than win his understanding; it seeks to annihilate rather than convert. Violence is immoral because it thrives on hatred rather than love. It destroys community and makes brotherhood impossible. It leaves society in monologue rather than dialogue. Violence ends up defeating itself. It creates bitterness in the survivors and brutality in the destroyers.

Exploring Possibilities

Let's use math as a way to master our mathematics skills. Let's use it to build our confidence and self-esteem and become more secure with ourselves. Remember, we are the beneficiaries of mathematics. We can use math in our relationships to explore the right approach before we speak. We have to organize our thoughts and actions. It can be difficult to solve problems and make proper decisions if we cannot make the right connections. Surrounding ourselves with the right types of people builds better relationships and positive connections. If a person's home lacks good communication or an important, close family member, it lacks organization, and it can be hard for that person to get back on track. That type of loss creates problems, including an unbalanced life and household because the person has lost connection with others. Many of us lost our way because we were miseducated and not taught how to apply lessons to life. If the curriculum had allowed the schools and teachers to teach math focused on connecting, growing, exploring, relationship, and order of sequences, math would be easier to grasp.

This is true of life itself. Math's main uses have been to explore science and to solve its many problems, whether through discussion or writing papers. Every day we explore many things about life through science and math and do not even know it. Every time we investigate, research, and experiment or experience something, we are exploring. The most important way we explore is through conversation and asking questions, but the focus is never on discussion. In conversation, we are exploring the many things we do not know, and most frequently, we ask questions in the hope of receiving the correct answers. Questions create mental word problems, and math is needed to solve them. These problems tell us the science; something exists along with requiring that we apply math to solve them or draw conclusions. Asking a question is a verbal word problem, or about reading comprehension; it requires thinking and an answer.

Asking questions of the wrong person and searching for answers in the wrong place are the same as not having an answer. We form questions, create them on paper, speak them in conversations, and explore them using our minds. The answers give us the math—its function, relation, connection, and sequenced order of how something happens to solve the problem. The concept of using math is through words, letters, and numbers in a certain order. All of us ask questions, and we are all explorers and scientists. Doctors explore to diagnose their patients' illness or conditions. Lawyers explore to solve cases. Students explore to learn so they can graduate to the next grade, and some teachers explore to find the best techniques to teach their student.

So why don't they teach word problems or allow questions to be asked daily? Why aren't they highlighted in the way we frequently use them, for life lessons? Many students have a hard time with math word problems and reading comprehension because there is no class that focuses only on questioning and because math and science are not taught together. Instead, the teacher tells the students that if they have any questions, to please ask them. This is clearly the main reason science and math should be taught together. Today, they are being taught separately when obviously they are made to be together.

Schools should teach math and science together and teach how to apply them in everyday life, so students can easily grasp the ideas. Instead, they are taught in long forms over about forty weeks a year for an average of thirteen years. For the most part, each subject has always been taught in its own classes and by its own teachers. This is also why most students have a hard time with reading comprehension, especially in mathematics. The curriculum most often used keeps us from knowing, understanding, and translating our purpose given to us by the Creator. If it had been taught properly, math would have been greatly appreciated and easily understood by all mankind.

Math explores the science of the equation for understanding and solves problems while seeking change. We human beings were created or brought forward to explore life and solve problems. Without them, we would be lost. Without problems, many of us would not function well, have a job, seek a job, or be interested in pursuing dreams and obtaining an education. Problems exist only to be solved, and there is no problem that cannot be solved. Businesses exist to solve certain problems. They hire employees to help them solve those problems, and in the end, everyone makes a profit, changes his or her life, and advances.

How can someone's problem become another person's problem over time, sometimes as much as hundreds of years later? Focusing on the past and blaming others does not advance a person, nor does it create a good change. I question the obvious daily: "Why do so many people claim to have suffered from certain problems that they were never there to experience?" I do not know. The past exists so we have something with which to compare the future. We are the beneficiaries of the past because we learn from mistakes. The past helps us make better decisions and calculate or estimate a successful plan of action. Without the past, how would we grow?

Many have forgotten how to apply knowledge to change their circumstances. Many do not know why they struggle in life. They do not understand life and their true purpose in it. Mainly, they do not know the Creator and His work. If they were taught that everything is science, is related to math, and is here for their own understanding, they would solve many of their problems and not be dependent on anyone. All things must be seen through the eyes of a scientist and explorer, which we are, but we have to know how to apply knowledge to better ourselves. Make them remember you and live your legacy. So if we do not learn from the past, we must learn from the present.

The biggest confusion with math lies within one's teaching, and if it is not taught correctly, with human purposes, it is useless. During an annual awards program for the youth, I often asked the participants which subject they had the most trouble in; the majority of them said mathematics. That is because the majority of the time, this subject is taught without application, or at least application isn't taught at the same time the basics are taught. For example, children who learn by seeing must see the math problem demonstrated with physical objects and have it related to science. If you give such students an equation with just numbers or without attaching it to visual objects or even pictures of graphs, they will have a hard time learning the idea behind the equation. They must be able to visualize it before they can apply or relate the idea to life. The only way they will learn the concept we have to teach them is the way the Creator intended for us to do it—by teaching the visual of how something relates and connects.

Understand that science is what we do or have been doing, and math is how we do it or how it can be done. Language is how we translate our story to later tell His-story—the story about the Creator, who is the author of life.

Part 2
The Life

Make Them Remember You

FIVE

Build a Legacy

A legacy is determined by how you live your life and what you leave behind that is of value to your inheritors. A legacy means making connections and building relationships; it means putting things in their proper place and removing what does not fit in your life. When you build a network of relationships that is positive, your life will thrive. The idea is to make sure your life is in order and you have organized it well. So whatever you have done with your life so far that has not helped you, do the opposite tomorrow.

Handle Your Business

For many years, we used our personal feelings to handle our business because we did not know business, finance, marketing, or ourselves. We stopped building ourselves up. We stopped searching for our own direction and purpose. We stopped searching for meaning in our existence. We even stopped contributing to the business within ourselves. Life is a business that we invest in; success depends on what we put into it. Every one of us was born with a business, and like any business, it is expected to grow and prosper. Our business is shown in the way we act, the way we speak, the way we dress, the way we look, and how we feel about ourselves and others. When we are unable to identify ourselves or make connections and relationships, many of us end up lacking confidence and not knowing how to apply these disciplines to our lives outside of figuring out how to add and subtract or how to dissect a frog.

To succeed in business, you create the business, market it and its products or services, operate it, and enjoy all the benefits of investing in it. If we take that same approach with our personal feelings and create out of them successful inner businesses, our lives will expand. The idea is to feed the mind with information that is relevant so we can make better choices instead of spinning our wheels in a morass of unruly, confused personal feelings. When we decide and act after careful reasoning and deliberation, we can feel confident in our choices, and the truth is not easily discarded if others find what we do offensive.

In life, we make friends, and in business, we cultivate clients. These relationships can elevate us to the next level, but if we don't control our personal feelings with wise minds and positive energy, our businesses will most likely fail. A goal in business is to treat people right because they are potential customers or supporters. If we treat them with respect, there is a good chance they will come back and continue to support us. A negative, disrespectful attitude can break a deal, turn away potential customers, and create all kinds of misery for ourselves and our businesses. Your customers do not care about excuses; they mostly care about what you have to offer them. It does not matter where you come from or what color you are; if you have something they need, they will buy it or trade with you.

Your appearance is another factor in succeeding in business; it means everything. If you are the one selling or providing the service, you must look the part to get the part. Look as if you already have it so that you can obtain it; have confidence and dress as if you are a success. The less you expose, the more respect you will gain. If you want the greatest outcome, you'll start with the greatest beginning. The science is to know that if you envision and follow a business system, you will go farther in life.

Business is not personal; it is an economic system that provides services and products. The more you provide or produce, the more you advance in those relationships. In business, it is not about you; it is about solving the problem of the business through you. Without problems, there is no gain. Your reputation is everything; it is the result of your work in dealing consistently with skeptics and believers alike. To receive a positive result, you must produce a positive attitude. No one wants to be caught doing business with someone who does not have solid business ethics or a good background or history. Behave so others will trust you. Always. If your reputation is good and it produces positive energy, mark my words: you will see the pot of gold at the end of the rainbow. As I said earlier, negative energy attracts negative energy. If you exude negative vibes, even if you try to hide them, people will pick up on it. They will not want to interact with you. Conversely, if you exude positive vibes and are true and sincere, people will respond positively to you. They will want to interact with you, and that is the key to success in business and in your personal life. This will also create a successful story and legacy.

To reap that reward, your reputation must hold value for others so they can see its worth. Showing yourself in a positive way—in how you dress and in your attitude—will get others' interest. Most of all, they will always remember you. The way you talk and the way you treat others holds energy and a lot of value. Your smile, your confident walk, and the professional way you dress attract positive people and hold value. Your kindness, patience, and confidence also have value, but it is up to us to define what each one of them is worth. A man's most valuable assets are his children, his talents, and his knowledge, which he can pass down to his children and their children. If we want to leave our children a meaningful legacy and wealthy future, we must take positive action now. So it is important that we carry ourselves tall so others will see the need to invest in our personal businesses—the professional and positive energy within ourselves.

What we have been taught but have failed to see is that every ethnic group that has come on its own to America has had a plan for building a future. Since we black people were forced to come, we did not have such a plan. As a black man living in America, I have seen the injustice of racism and witnessed the economic hardship that the government has caused for poor families and the uninformed. These things could have tainted my views, but I did not let them. I got through the negative; I applied a positive attitude and a sound understanding of where I fit into the world as an individual. I put in the hard work and sacrificed. And now things are different. There is nothing holding us back. To change our future, we must create a plan and learn how business works to achieve our goal of a better life. Now, we have a choice: we can conduct business using only uncontrolled, personal feelings, or we can use informed, organized minds. We decide. To succeed, we must learn to put our emotions aside to see the big picture calmly and reasonably. What will we gain from an emotional transaction that gets too personal? If you follow a realistic plan, you will learn to successfully market and operate your business and then enjoy all the benefits of investing in a successful business.

Whom should we blame if we approach a situation personally and let our emotions affect our growth? Whatever you want is yours through your own hard work and sacrifice. For you to become successful, you must prepare by acquiring the know-how, having the right mind-set, and taking the right approach. Make them remember you! All of us, no matter what color we are or where we come from, can operate our lives as businesses, being professional and rational while positioning ourselves for growth, or continue to fail by acting foolishly and thinking someone owes us something. If you think you received a raw deal, race and ethnicity will not matter: you will still be bitter. The business approach with a serious mind-set is the one that prepares us to be self-sufficient and free. This allows us to market ourselves in a professional manner, treating others as decent human beings or as potential customers by our ethical behavior.

Our personal business of being liable, trustworthy, self-respecting, and respectful is one in which we become the owner and the CEO of ourselves and our future. As for dreaming of a better life, it is an individual, private matter. We wait for the time when our efforts toward a realistic goal will succeed, but at the same time, we continue to work to realize our own dreams.

S I X

Be Prepared

Life is science, a system of rules, laws, and restrictions to keep things in order so that they function properly. For example, the human body has eleven systems, such as the nervous system and the immune system. Those systems also have rules, laws, and restrictions that keep our bodies running properly. Each system has a particular function and purpose. Every one of them needs to work in order for us to live, survive, and act appropriately. They require a certain sequence, method, concept, or connection. If we fail to give each one its proper requirements, we become deficient in that system, which can cause us to become sick or weak, or die. To avoid deficiency in any of the eleven systems, we must give our whole body proper and balanced care, such as fresh air, exercise, and healthful foods with sufficient vitamins, minerals, and other nutrients. The same is true of life. We have to find out what works based on our past and put all those things in motion. Life is a history book full of examples of what to do, so it is important that we be prepared and ready for the journey.

Know the Rules

Life has laws we must follow to make our lives better. God's laws of right and wrong and the laws of this land are instructions that people must follow to obtain the proper balance. If we refuse or act out in the wrong way, we will face consequences, which will keep us from advancing to the next stages in life. Clearly, we must follow the laws and systems for the same reason we follow them within our bodies—for a full, successful, and balanced life.

Rules to Life

> To whom respect is given it must be received.
> —Unknown

There will always be rules to follow, but many of us are not aware and do not know the rules for playing the game. If we want to win, we will learn the rules and follow them. The basic principle is simple: you have to learn the rules of the game before you can win. In any system, whoever understands the rules and follows the directions has a greater chance of advancing to the next level. To fix something, you must first know what is wrong. Some rules can be bent, but you need to know how far they can be bent before they are broken—and you are out of the game.

No matter how many times we try to deny it, the laws of the land are simply the laws, and there is no way around it. The laws we are supposed to abide by are made to protect us from others who would interfere with our progress and to protect others from our interference with theirs.

When you obey the laws, your ambitions and confidence can progress. You cannot commit a crime and think it will not affect you in a negative way. It will! Keep the math connected and positive. When your actions don't follow any principle, you will eventually fail, cause disruption, and damage a lot of lives unnecessarily. If you are not prepared to stand and face the obstacles and challenges in life or in history because you do not know right from wrong, you may lose your freedom forever. Respect the law and the police; their main purpose is to protect us. Someday, after all laws have been made, all games have been played, and all options have been tried, all of us will have to follow some type of rule.

Even in politics, our lives are being played out as a game, and politicians are testing us to see how we react. Almost everything that controls people is politically motivated. And because politicians write the laws, they control the present and future of America. It is our responsibility to learn the law, including the Constitution, the Declaration of Independence, the Bill of Rights, and what the Founding Fathers intended when they wrote them. We must also read and learn the Bible and its concepts. Whether you agree with them or not, they created the blueprint for how this country's business, or game, should operate. They explain how we should conduct ourselves and how they protect us so we can all grow, achieve prosperity, maintain good health, and pursue happiness. America is a nation of laws. The Creator is the governor of all laws. To advance in life, we must study the laws to be ready for the coming tests.

Recognize Life's Test

> In school, you're taught a lesson and then given a test. In life, you're given a test that teaches you a lesson.
> —Tom Bodett

Life is a series of tests, a system that examines and measures an individual's or group's skills, knowledge, intelligence, and capabilities. Every time we fail a test, our failure can give others more control over us. Life and its tests are a business with stock options—the more you know about how they work, the more freedom shares you earn. To win at life, you must know the rules, what it requires, and what is expected of you. Every test relates to the past. To pass a test, you must first study the rules, the manual, or the instructions. In any game, there are winners and losers. There are those who do not study, and there are those who do study. But no one can succeed without studying the rules unless it is by luck. Laws, rules, and instructions are the foundation for advancing in life, so do not roll the dice and lose your freedom.

When we were in school, many of us took many subjects for granted, mainly because we thought they served no purpose or were not important. But lately, they have come to be very important to our success. Now we are in a state of emergency, and we must take history and the laws seriously in order to grow. We must learn the laws to avoid the consequences of breaking them. Our greatest asset is knowledge, and the more we learn and the more we use that knowledge properly, the more we prosper. This plan is very simple. If we do not play to win, how can we win?

Be Responsible

America is the greatest country in the world, built on the belief that people can do anything and be anything as long as they follow the rules, work hard, and acquire the knowledge to put ideas into action. America was built to offer freedom to everyone who wants to live a good life, and it is the place where I have received that freedom. Although it has some flaws, no other country has ever offered people so much opportunity. But we have to beware of people who try to take our freedoms away. Being aware means knowing who these people are and connecting the dots to stop them. People risk everything they have to come here, including their lives. With the opportunities that come from freedom come the responsibility to protect that freedom. We have to be aware of the voices around us that are pulling us in different directions. The key to life is growing and prospering. How can we grow if our freedom is controlled by someone else? The Creator has given us life, talents, and the potential to succeed. But we must develop those gifts to build a happy, fulfilling life for ourselves and our families.

Most laws address freedom or certain protections, but not all laws were written for us to be free. America was founded on principles intended to protect our lives, freedoms, and religious beliefs as citizens of the United States as long as we abide by the laws. But in the event that we do not, we lose, and someone else profits from our mistakes. When we follow the rules, we flourish. Just as we are responsible for America as a nation, we are accountable for our own homes. And just as America was intended to depend on itself alone and not become indebted to any other nation, our objective is to take responsibility for ourselves.

The Constitution is one of the most important legal documents that we must know and follow, along with the Ten Commandments. Unfortunately, our rebellion has brought on terrible consequences. We have to accept America as our home, find what we are good at, and then pursue that talent or gift to make a living for ourselves and our families. I know many of us have struggled unnecessarily harder than others, but it will get better over time and with work from all of us. We must learn these laws and understand their worth and purpose to preserve our freedoms. I know America may not be the greatest country in the world yet, but it is the best one I know.

Our legacy and story involves knowing the laws of the land and the rules that protect our rights. By knowing and abiding by the laws created by the Founding Fathers, we all reap the greatest benefits—we prosper and remain free. These laws were made to protect our freedoms, including our right to choose our religion, and to protect us from interference by our government, a foreign country, any domestic body, or anyone else.

When you have a good understanding of America's laws and history, you can change your life. America is your home. Learn how to live in it. We have to let those who want to fight certain battles fight, but in the meantime, you must move forward with a better agenda, to feed and protect your family by using the laws of the country for your benefit. If you are a black American, like me, you have heard complaints from black leaders about how methods for our advancement thus far have not worked. That is mainly because not a lot of knowledge is being taught and passed down in the communities for growth. The ideas that could advance black Americans these leaders refuse to accept because these ideas eliminate them from the equation. But the methods people of other cultures have used have worked for them because they chose to follow a set of rules. These people understand language; they understand who they are, where they come from, and what their roles are in a new country. Having the key to a locked door is much better than kicking down a door with no key. The idea is to be prepared and follow the rules that will align you with succeeding. An old friend of mine by the name of Tanya Mitchell Graham once said, "Your life is of your own conscious decision."

So be prepared and make sure you know what you are getting yourself into before you lose your status and your freedom. The idea here is to know the rules and laws concerning whatever you do so that you never leave room for anyone to assume the worst of you. Otherwise you will end up in a place where freedom is not offered. So be ready and prepared to do what is right.

Know the Truth

There is absolutely nothing that we cannot do when we know the truth about God the Creator and follow His plans. Knowing truth is the prescription, the antidote, and the cure for our ability to have a truthful life. Truth is accurate, truth is real, and truth brings a halt to deception when it appears. Truth is consistent; it provides the level of integrity required of an honest person. When people's characters are developed in truth, their actions will reflect the sincerity of their hearts. Their actions will speak truth when they are honest. But if they do not recognize truth or they deny truth, the consequences become unbearable. Truth is pure and kind, and when it is sincere and honest, it is of God, the Creator.

Truth does not give false hope; neither does it give a partial picture. Truth gives the whole story, leaving nothing out. Truth is unchangeable; it is the only thing that we can believe in that is real. When there is truth, there is God's will. His truth lasts throughout all changes, forever and for all generations to come. It does not matter what color you are or how different you may be; if your character is not pure in truth, the content of your words and actions will be contaminated. Truth is the soul of freedom; it releases all doubt. It will never lead you astray. God's truth is calm, patient, and timeless.

Everything of substance is made of truth. Truth heals the sick, gives strength to the weak, and renews the soul of the soulless. There is nothing we cannot do when we have truth in our hearts. Even unbelievers will one day have to face the truth and pay a steep price for not believing and following the truth. Truth is knowledge; it prepares the unprepared. Truth will shine light to expose what is hidden in the dark. Truth is the only thing that is complete; it leaves a lying mouth closed after confrontation. In truth are everlasting love and hope. Truth infuses one with confidence in each trial on one's journey. It clears the path to prevent stumbling.

Truth does not make mistakes. It is always on time and on purpose. It does not create chaos; it restores order. Truth will never follow blindly but will acknowledge only that which is honest and pure. Truth is correct, it is flawless, and it does not make wrong choices. It analyzes, investigates, and provides facts for the benefit of the seeker. Truth is not always pleasant for the listener, and lying surely does not make the truth go away. Truth is light; it shows you what is right and wrong and then gives you the opportunity to make changes.

It is never too late to practice truth. It is ready when you are. The idea is to take it one day at a time. Walk if you are not ready to run, and sit if you are not ready to walk. Truth will sit and wait with you if you are tired; truth will let you rest. Just know it is not too late to embrace the truth, because when you are ready, He is waiting and would love to hear from you.

Start by reading a good book, or just be kind to yourself. Take time to evaluate where you are in life and start making plans to get to the next point. In all of this, love yourself and keep on hoping and planning. It is never too late to plant the seed; just make sure it will last long after you are gone. Some people never live to see the results of what they have planted. Lincoln planted the seed of freeing the slaves but never lived to see the results for those who accepted it. Dr. King planted the seed of love and equality but never got to see them accepted and fulfilled. So when you plant your seed, know you are planting it not just for you; you are also planting it for many generations that will come after you. It will not matter where you come from or who you are. Be strong; there is nothing you cannot do when you know truth and focus on it. Remember—your labor will not be in vain, because truth also provides immediate benefits:

- blessing
- sincerity
- salvation
- eternal life
- rest
- freedom of the mind
- gained trust
- gained honesty
- not having to remember a lie

Know Your Values

Who you are is not determined by what you have or, as Dr. King once said, not "by the color of your skin but by the content of your character." What you have does not mean anything if it is not embedded in the truth. Some people spend a lifetime attaching themselves to unworthy things that are poor substitutes for the truth. We are placed in this world to do great things that are honorable and just. Whether we do great things will depend on what we value and worship. Our greatness can be of value only when others benefit from our actions. Find what is worthy of honor; then study it and respect it by imitating it. Without principles that are honorable, the future of man will be lost. Whom we honor and imitate is also of great importance. We must evaluate both with all the honesty we can muster. Where there is no honor, there is failure. The prisons are full of people who were never taught to honor worthy people and worthy goals, so they live out the sad consequences of dishonorable lives. People's actions reveal whom they have chosen to honor once their lives are exposed for all to see, so it is important to choose wisely so others can remember the good in you.

If we have not carefully chosen worthy values to live by, we give deceivers an open season to hunt us down, misuse us, and destroy us. As long as we can be painfully honest with ourselves, truth will guide us wisely. No one can be fooled if he or she is aware of the foolishness and its consequences. What we focus on will define the path we travel. Losing sight of our destiny and choosing wrong values will leave us lost. Our values determine our destiny; therefore, it is important to be awake to every decision we make. Living out worthy values will make it easy for others to recognize our goodwill. A kind heart and caring soul will clearly show their roots. We are all God's children, imbued with His love to accomplish great things as long as we follow His plan faithfully.

Nothing is worth having if it does not come from a firm foundation of true constructive values. After all, what other kind of foundation or source could there be than one's creator? Make them remember you! Live your legacy now. America cannot survive if its citizens refuse to stand with its founders on what has always made the country great. Those things that are truly important and honorable will last a lifetime and beyond.

Note: Do not confuse having good, strong values with the science of business, which is the scientific study of economics and the managing of money through behaving, thinking, and communicating with others. Throughout history, business has been used to make money, establish peace, and create profit in many forms, including property, service, trading, and natural resources. The word *business* comes from the word *busy*, which is what you are when you work to become successful at business. It is best done by having good character, manners, and etiquette.

Be Professional

As parents, it is our business to train our children's minds to be businesslike, to think and act professionally, and to provide them with the best education we can give them. This includes at-home teaching about history and the Constitution, exposing them to different cultures, and enrolling them in different, enriching off-campus programs. It is part of our responsibility to stimulate their interest in science, math, and technology so they will be exposed to everything. It is our job to teach them proper manners, and how to treat others respectfully and communicate effectively with them. If we succeed in our parental roles, we will have made the best investment and created the best business ideas for them to succeed. The results will become our legacy, our business plan, with all of us being the beneficiaries, the managers, and the investors in this company of self.

Now, call it what you want and get emotional, but one thing is certain: we must keep our personal feelings out of our business if we are to succeed because business is still business and prosperity is the main goal. You can live your life in control of your business, or you can let others hold that control. Choose one.

Beware of Temptations

Avoid letting others tempt you to act out. Control your own destiny. First, you need to be professional, no matter what. Ask questions politely to get the best response. Always address others with *sir* and *ma'am*. Take a seat if told to do so, and never show signs of disrespect, even if you are the one being disrespected. If you owe someone, pay the person back. But if someone owes you, ask for it back like a gentleman or lady. It is hard to be compensated if you are confrontational. It is hard to tell which one is the fool when two people are talking loudly. Whatever you want is yours when you are being professional. It is hard for others to deny someone when the person is at his or her best. Let the good in you shine over their foolishness.

Your reputation is all you have; it is a profile of who you are. It helps others decide whether to become your friend and partner with you. Profiling is necessary; it is your passport to being successful. In business, clients will look at your reputation's profile to understand what you can do for them. They need assurance that you are the right choice for them—that you are professional, honest, and capable. When it comes to business, profiling is nothing more than a status report, like a credit report or a credit check for a car loan. Banks and loan companies need to know if you can afford the loan, have any debts, and are likely to pay their money back. Companies require a background check for most jobs. Before you rent an apartment, the owner requires your rental history. If you are seeking companionship through a dating service, it will need your profile to find the best match. If you are seeking a babysitting job, the parents of that child or children will need your profile, so be prepared to provide it. What others think of you can make or destroy your personal business. The stories they tell or think, based on your actions, create their perception of you. Your character defines your story—who you are and what you are capable of doing. The idea here is to know the science in you; that is who you are in life.

SEVEN

Our World

Science tells us who and what we are. What matters most is our purpose. But what we are made of is what makes our purpose so important. This is our world, made just for us. We are here, and we aren't going anywhere anytime soon. We are part of the universe, and everything used to create the world was used to make us. But we must know what is ours and can be accomplished before it is too late.

Our Abilities

When God created the universe, or caused it to exist, He made everything. All things that exist are also within you and a part of the universe. When God created the universe, He made all things out of matter and energy. As mentioned earlier, matter is everything around us and within us, in four observable states: solid, liquid, gas, and plasma. Nothing exists unless it has one of those characteristics. Each one of them either exists in you or was created for you. Remember the world belongs to you! Make them remember you! Everything that exists is matter and has energy. This includes the stars, planets, and galaxies, which are all normal matters of the universe and are made up in you.

When God created energy or caused it to exist, it was to show us how all things work. Energy generates, transfers, and changes form. It cannot be destroyed or created, but it is the key element that exists in you. Everything we see and hear has always existed. In physics, energy is the ability to do work. We can see energy in the forms of work and heat.

Anything, including you, that can move will create power, generate energy, and work. All work requires some type of action, a movement with energy that is never lost. In our everyday life, work is the basic requirement for achieving any goal. No work, no success.

As mentioned before, energy can be stored (potential energy) and available for motion or work, or it can be moving (kinetic energy) when we are engaged in that work. Work is an activity that involves movement and force. Energy has the ability to change forms, but it will not do anything until we make the decision to do something, such as change our own negative situations and circumstances. The power and strength from energy allows us to act. Energy invites possibilities. Every time we use our energy, we get closer to opportunities. Power generates opportunities when there is applied work, action, or an engagement of two or more objects. On earth, a person without power, a job, or a working skill will not work. The law of energy says a body at rest stays at rest, and a body in motion stays in motion. That is true in science, and it is true for us in life. When our body is at rest, we accomplish nothing, but when it is in motion, we can do great things and show what we are capable of.

Since energy is the ability to do work and power is the ability to do it, we are the energy and power performing that work. Understand that we are all powerful. The same things that are in us—atoms—are in two of the world's deadliest, most powerful weapons: the atomic bomb and the nuclear bomb. Many believe the world greatest scientist, Albert Einstein, is responsible for the existence of the atomic bomb because of his discovery of the relationship between mass and energy, shown in $E = mc^2$. Einstein's famous equation basically says there is tremendous potential energy in the mass of anything, even something as small as an atom.

We are all made atomic, strong, and powerful. What the atomic and nuclear bombs can do we can do in our own way. We are a spark, a blast, and fire on earth and in our lives. We hold great power within. With the right amount of energy to create the right kind of personal power, we can achieve anything for ourselves and our families. We are that boom that can change the world in a positive way. If we do not work, we gain no power and no control over our lives. We are energy, power, and heat. It is not by accident that we were made to do good work, because if we do not work with great intent, we will lose our power and our strength. No planet holds greatness as we do. The earth orbits the sun, but the whole world circles and revolves around us. Without us, no one would know anything about the planets or the sun. No galaxy can match our great potential as long as we are connected and willing to work. Our purpose is to achieve great things, but we must use our great potential so the outcome will have a positive effect on the world and on us when we are engaging with others.

Our Space

When God created space, He made it to hold everything and then placed it to cover every place, everywhere, wherever we are. Space has no end; it has no boundaries. Within and outside each one of us is a space of potential, and there are no limits to what we can do. We belong here! Humans continue to explore many areas throughout the unknown in an attempt to understand unlimited space. Space is everywhere and within everything in this universe. It is space that tells us how to locate someone or something, and if it doesn't have a location, it does not exist. Space helps us to identify and distinguish all things individually. Every inch of space on earth can be found on a grid coordinate that marks longitude and latitude and can indicate where an object is. Military personnel use this system every day to locate planes, soldiers, and equipment. Airports use it to help pilots navigate and to track planes to avoid crashes.

Space belongs to human beings. It surrounds our every move throughout life, it holds and separates everything, and most of all, it gives the location of where we are. An empty place is still considered space. Every person and thing has a location in space, so make sure you are not wasting precious space occupying your place. We are all a part of space and are physically in space on earth. (Gravity keeps us from floating away and was made to keep us in place.) Space is what separates all things, even inside the body. Even the organs in our body have a place in space. Nothing exists without space. Space covers, contains, and surrounds all.

Atoms occupy space, just as atoms are in you. Atoms make up matter, and all things that have matter have mass. Mass refers to the shape and size of things. Without mass, the human body would not have weight, form, or detail. All mass, which is matter, takes up space. We matter to every space we take up and to wherever we are.

Greatest Stars

Each one of us is a walking universe, born like stars, planets, and the galaxy, held together by gravity and cosmic streams, and placed together perfectly. We were born to shine like the stars and be together like the planets and galaxies. In the galaxy are a gazillion stars, and on earth, there are billions of people. We are those stars; we create our own energy, held up by our own gravity to shine. We are the ball of gas that takes up space and produces our energy. The universe belongs to us.

Within the core of every star, including the sun, is iron and heat. Iron is produced when the core of the star gets extremely hot. Just like the core in humans, it is hot. Iron is a mineral that creates energy and assists our red blood cells in sending oxygen to the rest of our bodies. (As my son would say, "If there is iron in us, we must be the first Iron Man.") People's normal body temperature is 98.6 degrees Fahrenheit, and anything over 102 degrees Fahrenheit is dangerously high and usually needs a doctor's attention. Even the word *star* when applied to a person indicates excellence and greatness. Anytime you call a person a star (not just related to appearing in movies), it raises his or her confidence and defines the person as someone with high standards and stability.

The question is, How hot does it have to be before we realize it is time we use our energy to change our lives if they are troubling? Think about it.

If the Creator can hold the universe in place, surely He can hold us up with no mistakes. We are the stars of this universe. The earth is our stage, and we are the performers on that stage who were selected to live under the big lights. The Creator has made every star an image of Him. As it says in Psalm 82, "You are gods, sons of the Most High." No cosmic stars can shine more brightly than we do. We are like planets revolving around each other's energy and designated space. So it is important that we take the stage and shine where we are before our own light goes out.

Our Spirit

In the beginning when the Creator brought man into existence, He gave him life and spirit, the same thing as in the universe. In the Bible, the word *spirit* can refer to breath and life, but as we humans know, breath consists of nothing more than the air we breathe. That same air we breathe, or spirit within us, surrounds the earth in layers and makes up the atmosphere. Remember this is all for us. The atmosphere is what controls the earth's temperature. During the day, it protects the earth from being burned by the sun's rays, and at night, it traps the heat on earth to keep it at a relatively moderate temperature for us. No forms of life exist without the spirit, air, or breath, and without people, none of them exist, because people are the ones all of this is truly for. The spirit is also the animator, the life force, the energy force of the body. Once the body stops breathing, the air stops moving through the lungs, and life stops. This means that as long as there is spirit in you, you have a chance, so do not give up. Just live your legacy!

The spirit is like the invisible electric current that flows through a machine. Our spirit, or the breath within us, is our movement or driving force of energy that gives us life, indicating the God within us. It charges the whole body, especially the brain. Without a brain, breath, air, or any spark of life, it is impossible to live. However, when the body is dead, technically we are not. Our bodies' remains transfer energy and change form into a different kind of energy; whether burnt ashes or dust, the body still exists and is not dead, just as we are not dead. However, when our bodies are declared dead, the spirit or life force goes back to the Creator while the remains end up someplace on earth. No matter what, we still exist. Even many of the organs can be transplanted to other people who are already living, so the recipients can live longer in this lifetime rather than starting a whole new life. This amazing fact makes us the greatest creation known in the universe. If you ever think your life is over or does not matter, think again. Understand also that one of the most important times in our lives is when breath and spirit are within us, so do not take your life for granted while you still have it.

All over the world, the Creator lives, for He is the life of the universe. He is also known as the spirit of the universe. Life and spirit are the presence of all things that exist, which means the Creator has brought them all into existence through the life of humans and recognized by our senses. Everything that exists or is present in time has life, as long as humans exist, it has either breath or air, it has a name, and most importantly, it serves a living purpose.

When people or things pass away, the last things that exist besides their energy are their purpose, spirit, and name; as long as we hold the dead in memory or say their names, their spirit and purpose live on. Many great people are still living today in our memories, by the grace of their spirit and the speaking of their name. Even our loved ones, family members, and friends who are not here in flesh are still living today by the speaking of their names and the spirit. Christians believe Jesus died on the cross and his name, purpose, and spirit live on and live in many of us. His mind, body, and soul continue, as long as we recognize his existence. He exists and lives on within us as the Holy Spirit.

This is also why it is important that we call each other by a name that is positive, especially our children. Whether it is a nickname or their birth name, calling them by a positive name builds their confidence and gives them something to live up to while speaking their legacy into their mind. Even today, I call my own children by names that can help build their character or bring strength to their weaknesses. I called my oldest son, Justice, "the Great Jay," and my youngest son, Austin, "Mr. Awesome," in the hope they would one day live up to their name, purpose, and existence in righteousness and spirit.

The spirit is energy in one's conscience, the work of God that helps us make everyday decisions. The spirit is also known as the Holy Spirit. Growing up, I heard many pastors tell their congregations to speak to the spirit in a person to help them make better decisions. What they are trying to do is speak to you, your conscience, to bring a better person into existence. What they may not know is that they are attempting to try to transfer a negative spirit into a positive one or to change the energy of a person from potential to kinetic. Remember *potential* means you are in an idle position, doing nothing; *kinetic* means you are moving, doing, and making things happen. In other words, your life is not over until breath leaves your body or you stop working to make things happen. There is a chance for all of us to become great and awesome, but the focus should be on making that happen right now and not later. We are alive with a purpose and have plenty of time to discover it and make changes as long as we have breath in our body.

Our Earth

When the Creator brought earth into existence, He gave humans total control over it, making them His greatest discovery. The Creator has made everything on earth for people. Trees are the biggest plants in the world, and they need water. Everything depends on it. Trees keep our air clean—they give off oxygen and water and take in harmful carbon dioxide so that all living things can breathe. Their roots keep the soil from washing away. Their trunks provide water, food, and protection for animals, insects, birds, and other plants to grow and live. And trees provide lumber for people to build homes. Because of water, people have used the trees to also make paper, shoes, and all sorts of products.

Earth was made for people to live. Doors are made for people to open. Dirt was created for people to use to build foundations and grow crops. Words are made for people to read, write, and comprehend. Everything we see is for us to see, everything we hear is for us to hear, and everything edible is for us to live. Everything you see is for people; everything that exists is for us. If all things are for us, why can we not master doing things right to feed ourselves and our families? If people did not exist, there would be no one to create ideas, solve the many problems, or improve on them. We have made this world advanced throughout all forms of life. No other species has such great power and influence. We have explored many parts of earth, as well as distant space. We have transformed the little into greatness. We have taken trees, metal, and stones to build homes, roads, buildings, and bridges. Where we once used our feet to travel, we now have bikes, cars, trains, and airplanes. We have made wonders out of earth, just as the Creator has done wonderful things with us. This is why we must continue to explore and use our minds to find understanding.

Our Water

Water is one of the simplest things we've been given and that we've explored. The chemical formula for water is H_2O, which is made up of two of the most basic elements on earth, hydrogen (the H in H_2O) and oxygen (the O). (The symbol H_2O for water means a water molecule has two atoms of hydrogen and one atom of oxygen.) Every human being is about 60 percent water. Just as there is water in our bodies, it is in the earth—its surface is about 71 percent water. It is also in the air in the form of a gas, water vapor. Water is changed into water vapor by evaporation; then it rises to form clouds. In liquid form, water is lakes, rivers, oceans, rain—what the Creator used to supply the Garden of Eden and to create four rivers, where He placed man after he was formed. Water takes on solid forms as snow, sleet, or hail. Water is the major part of food for all living things. People and everything they need require water to stay alive. Without water and its elements—hydrogen and oxygen—in man's body, he could not survive. Everything needs oxygen, hydrogen, and water. Without them, there would be no food. Even animals need them to serve their purpose on earth, including as food for humans or as pets (as less talkative friends). Since the day of creation, man has hunted animals for food and used their skin and fur to keep warm.

Humans are the reason water from rain is used to make mud and clay, which together hold trees up and keep their roots in the ground. God used even the dust and clay the earth was created with to create man. People use that same dust and clay to build homes and buildings out of stucco, brick, and stone. Everything that needs water has helped humankind advance. Water nourishes all.

Our Food

Without people, there would not be any need for water, there would be no food chain of animals, birds, and insects, and there certainly would not be any need for nuts, fruits, vegetables, or plants to make medicine. Eating green vegetables, such as kale and cucumbers, all types of beans, avocados, hazelnuts, almonds, and sea salt especially helps our growth. The main purpose of life is growth, and without it, nothing prospers. Over the years, man has used many plants and herbs to make medicines to cure diseases.

People are the reason for water in the oceans, rivers, and lakes; those bodies of water were created to feed living things in them and around them all over the world. People are the reason those same bodies of water were created to hold animals, so we could have another food source. The Creator purposely created certain fish and many other sea animals with nutritional elements and compounds that the human body needs to function. Fish and other kinds of seafood contain protein, essential amino acids, and omega-3 fatty acids, so they are especially good food sources for us. Just about all the main elements of an amino acid are needed by our bodies—oxygen, nitrogen, carbon, and hydrogen. And omega-3s are good for the human brain and memory. You can clearly see that fish and many other animals have what our bodies need to grow and survive.

Equally Unique

We are all one when we accept the Creator. We are the human race, and each of us connects with everyone else in mind, reality, and spirit. All of us were made for this. Every one of us was given the right talent, the right height, the right character, the right amount of intelligence to make the right decisions, the right everything to succeed in life. Nothing holds us back. We are all stars; we shine and matter. We take up space, and we are the solid that produces liquid and gas. It is not by accident that we were made the way we are. Everything is uniquely connected and exists to keep us growing, evolving, and equally connected.

It is not by accident that adults usually have thirty-two teeth to help them talk and chew to break down food. It is not by accident that we are here. All of us were given an equal number of everything (arms, feet, ears, and so on), and they exist in the same location on our bodies beginning from the day of conception. How else would our ears automatically know to place themselves on either side of our head so we can listen to each other? How else would our eyes align evenly on our face so we can see each other's greatness? How would our mouth know to place itself at the bottom center of our face? And how would our hands and legs be placed evenly on both sides of our body? Each of these features has a purpose and is placed on each one of us in a superb and dynamic way. Each sense and body part clearly has something of a brain and mind of its own. Something connects them and makes them function consistently—nerves, joints, and ligaments, not to mention atoms, cells, and energy, just to name a few.

We were placed in this universe in the most excellent position. The World Belongs to Us! We are all created and made to be together and connected somehow. Each of us consists of energy that was transferred and changed form from the friction of both parents, from the sperm of our father and the egg of our mother. This is the system of reproduction and the only way life works and can grow. If the theory of creationism is true, the Creator took His time creating woman. He made her unique and special. "He put man asleep to create her and used man's ribs to form her," which makes her tailor-made and perfect. This is the reason the devil dislikes woman so much. She is the life and helper to all. Believe it or not, the woman is goddess, Mother Earth, and nature to the world and to humankind. She must be honored for this and treated with respect at all times. Everything feeds from her. In certain black communities, the grandmother holds the family together. In other ethnic communities, the glue that holds families together is different. The woman is the one who keeps the family together and maintains the home, and she is the one to whom we all are drawn. Nothing would exist if not for her nurturing and the bond, connection, and energy she has with her family or man on earth, for this is how God created all things to work.

Women and men are the breeders for all civilizations and cultures. Even in the early periods when men came and conquered new land, their mating with the native women started civilizations of new people and cultures. Woman was purposely made from man and for man, and man was made to create life and build a family with woman. There is no other way it works. Any other way would stop the flow of life.

Universal People

Each of us is a universe of unity—one language, one sound, and one vibration to form one communication. In language, we are the subjects of every sentence spoken and written about us, especially those that highlight our actions. We are the verb in every act with which we engage. We are a vision that all have planned to see. Even the word *universe* is unique and special. The first part of the word, *uni*, means "one," and the second, *verse*, from the Latin *versus*, means "turned." When you put them together, it means "turned into one whole." The Creator is both—the center and the whole, the one who holds all.

The same applies to the word *science*. It comes from the Latin *scire*, which means "to know" and must refer to the Creator, who is the source of all knowledge. However, many would give science, rather than the Creator Himself, the credit for all knowledge. The Creator has given us life and the ability to accomplish great things together in our extraordinary bodies on earth, but we have to understand how important we are and how important our purpose is. We are science connected by our gifts, existence, and nature to keep all good things up to par because everything the universe was created out of was created for us—for every man, woman, and child.

We must understand that God is the Creator of everything; He created or brought forward everything for us so we can solve problems, or at least be on a path to search for solutions. Problems are opportunities. The only way you can fail is if you choose not to solve a problem or follow a law. All of this is science, that is, knowledge. But we have to be smart enough to use this knowledge and nature, and to know the Creator has given us all we need to survive. We are all leaders, in charge of our own lives and this world. There are all sorts of reasons why life is the way it is and why the universe exists, so let us embrace the world's positive energy. The world belongs to us. Make them remember who we are. This is our story, and it is time we live our legacy now.

EIGHT

Take It Further

Knowledge is something we store in our memories to use at a later time. It is our database of information, stored in our own human computer. What we put in and what we tell our computer to remember will be all that it knows. How far will it go if we are not putting anything into it? What happens when we have nothing else to put into it, and how long will it last? Remember this is your story, where you decide the ending. If you are limited in your thinking, you will become limited in your life. The idea is to take your mind and your knowledge further, far beyond where your human computer can go.

Your Mind

The most important organ in the human body is the brain. The word *brain* is often substituted for the word *mind*. The brain is a physical thing, whereas the mind is mental. The mind usually refers to thinking, remembering, intending—what the brain does. The brain is responsible for a variety of functions and controls the science of everything we do. It stores information and allows us to think, draw conclusions, and reason, much like a computer. We are taught to think, and a computer is programmed to process. We are given orders, and a computer is given commands, but we are in control of it all. Just as a computer has hardware and software, we have a brain, the hardware, and a mind, the software.

Protect your mind; don't let anyone try to control it. Your dreams live there. No one should have access to your mind. The mind is the database of stored thoughts and ideas that is ready to be put to work. When the mind does not process any data, it is always because we have not given it data to consider, and we have not let it expand its capabilities beyond our wildest beliefs. Our brains require information to expand. Every time we take in information, it is stored in our minds until our brains send signals to retrieve it. However, when nothing is there, our brains do not respond. And when there is no response, anger or fear result. This is why we must protect our minds at all costs. Our minds are the only things we can control until we share their contents with others. Others can claim our thoughts as soon as we speak or write them if we are not careful and prepared. To protect our minds, dreams, and thoughts, their written or spoken forms must be copyrighted or trademarked. This process guarantees our ownership with exclusive rights to that database. As soon as we pull a dream from our thoughts, its journey takes its course. The Creator has given each of us the ability to dream. Our private thoughts in our dreams must be protected before we release them into the world.

Some people play tricks with our minds by using them against us. They show us only what they want us to see, play only what they want us to hear, and pack stores only with food they want us to eat in the hope of controlling us and making us dependent on them. Do not let them! Protect your mind; your future also lives there.

To become rich, you must protect what can make you rich, and that is your mind. Over the last few decades, we have given away our dreams and ideas with no pay or advancement. We have given everyone the opportunity to exploit us and take our dreams away. Our dreams are the foundation of our personal business, but negative information that is shared can be used against us. Ears that are near can overhear it, social media can spread it, and predators who lurk can take our dreams away from us. Hackers can use our thoughts, conversations, and emails to destroy our reputation. So do not empower anyone else's career with your dreams and ideas. Be mindful about the media. They will claim they are giving you an outlet to let your voice be heard. Media outlets such as radio stations will delude us with claims that they are providing an outlet for us to free our minds. In reality, we are freely giving away our business ideas so that others can make money. You do not know them, and technically, they are strangers. They mean only to solicit our information so they can build their business. Supporting someone's business is one thing, but destroying yours in the same act will never make you rich.

Our mind is where our dreams wait for us to direct its path and destination. No matter what we may think, no two dreams or journeys will be the same. Dreams give us our own identity and set us apart from others. They separate us creatively from one another and make each of us special. So protect your dreams and be careful when you release them into the universe because you might lose ownership of them.

People who may have less in the material sense need to stay focused. The quickest way out of poverty is a job and education. A job gets you out of poverty, and education sends you to the next level. Having a good education and a job requires work; no work, no progress. Humans' purpose is to progress, work, grow, and gain knowledge. Knowledge is meant to be learned, stored, taught, or transferred. The reason to seek knowledge is to gain understanding. The purpose for wisdom is to expose what is wrong in life. To gain wisdom, one must study differences and understand concepts. We are our minds and thoughts. What consumes us is within us. The brain holds the mind, and it must have positive movement for you to succeed. If the mind is not moving—processing thought, learning, and holding knowledge—it most likely will not work properly.

Whatever enters the mind will affect what we do and become for the rest of our lives. Monitor what goes in or you will regret it. In your mind is the system of science that is ready to work. No success has ever been achieved without the use of the mind and the effort of hard work. Your mind is a series of mental processes, operations that allow your whole body to act. The mind generates a series of actions, steps, and motions that lead to results. It discovers ideas given to you by God. Your mind is a mass of energy that is made to perform a task.

Imagination

The biggest threats to many people have been their inability to think for themselves, their lack of knowing their scientific purpose, and their failure to see what they are capable of doing. These deficiencies have allowed others to think and talk for them and their families in the worst way. But if people only knew how great they are and acted on it, their intelligence would increase far beyond what they can imagine. If you ask yourself questions that a person cannot answer, it is probably because that person has no imagination.

You receive knowledge when you use your imagination. Imagination is what you use when you think and visualize outside the norm or the present reality; you see things beyond their original purpose and time of existence. Our imagination helps us formulate new ideas and images after understanding the old ones. When we use our imagination, we are seeing things outside our human experience or outside that so-called box.

According to Jess Brallier's book *Who Was Albert Einstein?* Einstein once said, "Imagination is more important than knowledge. Knowledge is limited. Imagination encircles the world." What is in our minds is stored memory and the knowledge of everything we have sensed—seen, heard, and experienced—in life. But the things we have not can be explored or found in our imagination. Everything we know, who we are, and what we will become consumes our minds and our imagination. Our minds hold the knowledge we have obtained. The mind determines our actions, how we make decisions, and how we live our lives.

Every decision we make reflects our imagination. Before a teacher ever gained the knowledge to become a teacher, he or she imagined life as a teacher. Before a lawyer was a lawyer, he or she imagined life beyond the present. Both needed imagination to create a dream, set a course to follow, and keep in mind the goal: to become a teacher or a lawyer. Success must be imagined before it can be accomplished. Imagining gives a vision to aim for. People's titles describe who they are and the knowledge they obtained. But their imagination gives them the vision to see just how far they can go and how creative they can be. These people used their brains to think and imagine their lives outside that so-called box. Imagination is a spiritual connection and communication with the Creator; He gives us every image, vision, and idea. Therefore, we can say imagination is having the ability or the power to create images and ideas in one's mind.

One day, I asked my nine-year-old son, "What is an imagination?"

He replied, "Your thoughts."

"What is knowledge?" I then asked.

He gave the most common definition: "Knowledge is in everything."

"So what did Einstein mean in his comment?" I asked.

My son did not know.

I said, "If we look at all the things in a room, there is knowledge and information about everything in it. Each thing has a purpose, even those things in the room we cannot see."

"What do you mean?" he said.

I replied, "The air in the room. You can't see it, but we know it is in here along with everything else, and without it we would not be here."

We perceive everything in the room. Everything has mass and energy; all that exists possesses knowledge and information. But only when you see and discover why they exist do you understand what else they can do on another level or for another purpose. For example, credit cards were created for us humans to eliminate carrying cash, for customers to buy expensive items without formally taking out a loan, and for financial institutions to make money on borrowed money at high interest rates. However, some people used their imagination and figured out how to use those cards to open locked doors. (I do not condone breaking the law, but if criminals were to see past the crime and use their imagination in a positive way, many of them would be better citizens and great inventors instead of sitting behind bars or dead.) The lesson here is to see past the original purpose of things, uncover a new one, and succeed by simplifying life or making money from your insight and creativity. What comes easily creates the best life. It is best if people see themselves doing what they love or what comes to them easily so they can achieve great things.

Practice Thinking

There is an old saying, "practice makes perfect," and it's true. The dictionary at merriam-webster.com defines *practice* as "do[ing] something again and again in order to be better at it." That is what people who excel at something do—they practice over and over again, become good at it, and then become a professional in the field and start making money doing it.

But many were never taught to practice thinking, to practice using their minds. When you practice something physical, you are rehearsing, trying, learning, winning, and succeeding at it. When you practice thinking, you are concentrating, focusing, imagining, and using your mind. The more you practice thinking, the more you will imagine seeing your future or visualize reaching a goal. Practicing is necessary; it is how we reach our highest potential. The more we imagine and practice, the more we increase our chances of success and build our confidence. The same is true for all activities.

One of the main reasons we practice or study is that we do not completely understand God's work. Often a person practices or studies because he or she does not have a full understanding of why something exists. Or the person may want to educate himself or herself further. A doctor is said to practice medicine because he or she does not know or understand God's creation of nature or His science of medicine in its entirety. Remember the doctors diagnose the problems but we tell them what they are. The only true doctor is the Creator. He is the doctor of all doctors, and we are the students of medicine, the scientists and explorers who study the subject. This is why when you are having certain kinds of surgery or undergoing certain operational procedures, you may first be asked to sign a waiver—in case something goes wrong. Hospitals and doctors do not want you to hold them accountable for what they are practicing and trying to understand.

The more those studying to become doctors practice or repeat their lessons, the better they get. At some point, they have imagined becoming a doctor. Actually, they are practicing understanding God's work, His science of medicine. The same is true for lawyers. The more they practice law, the better they become in understanding it—how judges interpret the law, how laws are applied to citizens, what specific laws mean—and understanding God's laws, which include the laws of the land and political science.

For instance, a married couple's assignment from the Creator is to reproduce. They practice reproduction by becoming affectionate with each other before conceiving a child, but it is still practicing. If our parents had not imagined a child and then conceived us, we would not be here.

None of these outcomes exist without people using their imaginations and practicing their futures in the present. Practicing makes us better at reaching our goals, satisfying our desires, and using our unique abilities. But we must first know what we can and cannot do to make the best out of life. Then we can seek out the best with our years of experience and a great reputation.

Taking It Further

Talk to Yourself

For years, we have been told not to talk to ourselves because it will look as though we are crazy, foolish, or not intelligent. One reason many people have said talking to yourself makes you seem crazy is that they want to talk to you. They are trying to spread corrupt knowledge to advance their cause. They want to be the only one feeding your mind. They do not want you to get ahead without them guiding your thoughts. What they do not tell us is how important it is to recognize negative self-talk, that inner dialogue we have with ourselves throughout each day. They do not tell us how important it is to turn negative self-talk into positive self-talk. They also do not want to tell you that your self-talk is brainstorming, thinking out loud, and educating yourself.

In the process of talking to yourself, you are listening, learning, and thinking. When you start talking to yourself, questions come up that require answers that you need to think about. Your brain starts to analyze a question and search to find the answer, and after carefully thinking and reasoning, arrives at one. This process is also called practical thinking, critical thinking, or being open-minded with yourself because you are applying reasoning and logic. Talking to yourself or questioning yourself invites your imagination to investigate, think, and research; then your mind draws a conclusion. Your talking to yourself is a threat to certain people—enemies, politicians, leaders, or anyone who does not want you to succeed on your own. Certain classes of people do not want you to talk to yourself because you will start solving your own problems and start building trust in yourself.

Talking to yourself is an art, or a technique, that builds confidence, focus, self-esteem, and courage. When you pray to your God, you are talking to yourself, hoping He hears you. Many believe that the more you pray, the better your chance of being heard by God. Talking to yourself teaches you how to focus; it tunes everything out around you. It creates a quiet time for yourself. The only thing you hear during that moment is yourself thinking and breathing. When you are talking with yourself, you are in deep thought or meditation, searching for an answer to a problem. Even doctors, whose job is to solve medical problems, talk to themselves, especially when taking notes. Some men and women with the greatest minds have talked to themselves while creating inventions and running countries. Albert Einstein, Thomas Edison, Ronald Reagan, George Washington Carver, Lewis Latimer, Dr. Martin Luther King Jr., and many others all, at some point, I believe, talked to themselves. If an idea ever arrived in their thoughts spontaneously, they talked to themselves. If they even rehearsed a speech in the mirror or by themselves, they talked to themselves.

When you talk to yourself, you ask questions, open your mind to new possibilities, and present opportunities for your mind to solve. You cannot get anywhere or solve any problem until you start asking questions. Even when you pray, you are self-consciously talking to yourself and asking questions, although the only voice you hear asking and answering is your own. Some have said, "Praying is positive thoughts," but if it is spoken out loud, it is talking. Ask yourself questions! Answers solve problems; without a solved problem, there is no gain. Problems lead to solutions and rewards.

Dependence starts when you do not think for yourself. The enemy wants you dependent and not thinking for yourself because you might stray from the path the enemy wants you to follow and then lead your own life. The enemy knows that once you start talking to yourself or asking yourself questions, your mind will start searching to find the answers, and later you will no longer need others to guide you—you will be able to guide yourself. Your conscious decisions determine the life you have. So make sure you ask the right questions to get the best answers.

If you are not asking any questions, you will never get any answers. Answers are all around us, but if we don't ask any questions, we ignore them and fail to connect them in their right place. If you are not asking any questions of yourself or others, you will never know where the answers belong. Questions and answers go together; they are partners and in deep relationship with each other. But the moment you have no more questions on a topic or cannot find the answers, you have reached the limit of the knowledge you can get from your conversation with yourself, and the self-talk on the subject ends.

Thinking is God's greatest gift to humankind, but because people are accountable for what they say and do, they should think five times before they speak or act. People who do not think do not gain the knowledge to advance in life. Those who wait to speak look wise. Thinking prepares the tongue for words. Talking without thinking creates gossip. Thinking creates focus and exercises the brain to become better at focusing.

Talking to yourself teaches you about yourself and how to process thoughts. Every time you talk to yourself or ask yourself questions, the process automatically activates your mind to start thinking of answers. Talking to yourself is good because it leaves you curious and desiring to know more and solve problems. If a person is never curious about something, most likely he or she will never gain the desire to learn more on the subject or try to achieve anything. Self-talk helps the mind to develop, become full of knowledge, and be used. People who do not think to themselves (or think out loud) will always rely on others to think for them; it is the nature of life. That is why you must talk to yourself.

When you talk with yourself, you are discussing topics that are relevant only to you. In most cases, they are what are important to you at that moment and about something that happens before your self-questioning begins. You start to analyze what you are experiencing at that moment—maybe in response to something that just happened. In many cases, it is about a matter you do not understand or have enough information about. Nevertheless, it is something dear to you that must be discussed and solved.

We all talk to ourselves. Some of us might need to practice in front of a mirror to recite a speech or lines in a play. We may get angry with someone and find, even after that person is long gone, that we are talking to ourselves while imagining that person is still in front of us. We might use swear words, but we are still just talking with ourselves.

The more we practice talking to ourselves and in front of a mirror, the more passionate we become—enough to envision the best future and make changes to bring that vision to life. There is absolutely nothing wrong with talking to yourself and asking yourself questions to get answers. Some people talk to themselves to envision success. Take a little boy outside throwing a football up in the air. In his mind, he sees himself making a big play, so he shouts, "Touchdown!" The boy is talking success to himself. His mind is practicing and rehearing success over and over. Remember practice makes perfect.

Muhammad Ali got beat up every day, but after hours and hours working in the gym and talking to himself, he became a legend in boxing. Take a woman reading a recipe and, in talking to herself, discovering that she has left something out. If she had not talked with herself, she would not have known what she forgot. Talking to yourself helps you succeed.

In school, teachers sometimes ask students to read quietly or to themselves, just so they can hear themselves think in order to comprehend what they are reading. The teachers are also getting the students to focus and pay attention. How many times have you said something ridiculous or stupid out loud and later wondered why you spoke those words? But if you had never responded to your thoughts, you never would have realized that you misspoke, which helps you learn not to repeat what you said. If you had not questioned yourself, you would never have known your mistake.

You already think to yourself. Make it a habit to talk to yourself. Start asking and answering harder questions and see your mind begin thinking and processing knowledge inside and outside the box. If you are not talking to yourself, you are not thinking and learning about yourself and your life. If you are not talking to yourself, you are not thinking; you are wasting valuable personal time instead of doing things that you may not know your mind can do.

You are told to read to yourself, so tell me why you cannot talk to yourself. There is no difference! When you want to know someone, what is the first thing you do? You talk with that person. So talk to yourself to get to know you! You do it anyway. Anytime you are by yourself and words are coming out of your mouth, you are talking to yourself through thought. If you are singing and start to get into the song with emotions, you are talking to yourself through thought, rhythm, and sound. The words of the song are stimulating your brain, causing you to physically connect with the words and the vibration of the beat. The beat sends signals to help you make a quick connection with the words. If fact, singing to themselves was how slaves connected with God and the hope and promise of freedom, which they later received. So go ahead and get comfortable talking to yourself; nothing crazy will happen. Just remember that when you talk to yourself, you are really talking to your conscience, the Spirit, the God in you. Success is in you. Go get it and live your legacy now. He is with you.

Gossip to Yourself

Talking to self is also gossiping. Although many say we should not gossip, I believe we should, although mostly to ourselves. Gossiping is a discussion at idle position, a conversation or rumor about someone or something, but when you gossip to yourself, there is no trace of harm. Gossiping teaches us and helps us understand things and one another, but gossiping to others with no proof can create all types of problems. As long as it is guiding our conscience to a positive and productive outcome, there is nothing wrong with gossiping, especially to ourselves. Ultimately, gossiping is simply conversation that involves exchanging information and ideas with a person or group. So if it is acceptable to talk with others, then there should not be anything wrong with gossiping and talking to ourselves. Gossiping makes you think and investigate before presenting facts. It is using common sense and logic, which we should always do.

If you do not understand something, gossiping or talking with others can help you get a better perspective on the matter. Just be careful not to cause problems by responding to rumors about other people. Gossiping requires focus and questions and answers. During the time a person is gossiping, he or she is concentrating, processing his or her thinking, and analyzing for a better understanding. When people talk to themselves or gossip, they tune out everything around them. They place their mind in that idle or concentrating position to gather more evidence, which starts the thinking process.

Gossiping is done in every board meeting and conference, before, during, and after every game among teams and fans, and among those who spy for advancement. If it is right for people to gossip in those contexts, why is it not okay for you, especially if you are gossiping about an enemy or simply to advance yourself? Gossiping enables you to think to yourself, solving problems and finding answers on your own. Over time, we have gotten answers for ourselves, just as we have gotten answers from one another. We have solved many of the same problems by self-talking, gossiping, using reasoning, and drawing logical conclusions.

Go ahead: talk to yourself about yourself. Let yourself know where you have gone wrong and what you need to do to correct any problems you might have. Start gossiping with yourself, tell tall tales about yourself and your plans to be successful, and then do everything in your power to live up to them. Do not be afraid of being real with yourself; tell yourself about the good qualities you don't have and make it be the talk of your personal mental town. Start a rumor about how smart you are and how great of a success you're going to become, and live it out. Gossip to yourself about how you want to be the doctor who will save thousands of lives after you graduate from medical school. Gossip to yourself about your dream of being the president and then make it a reality. Gossip with yourself. You already gossip with others.

Be Nosy about Yourself

People should be nosy about themselves, for it is observation—the act of observing or paying attention. The best way to learn about yourself is to pay attention to yourself. When people are nosy, they are looking deep into a matter or subject. They are also analyzing, focusing, and paying attention to what they put their mind on. Being nosy is a good trait we all should have. People take into account what they see, hear, and question. Nosy people are eager to know, learn about, and understand the world around them. They also investigate and research the gossip and take their time trying to get to the bottom of a situation. When they have gathered enough information and are ready to draw their own conclusion, the nosiness stops. Some would say nosy people are snooping or in other people's business, but I say they are just doing their research and paying attention.

Many people do not want you to be nosy with yourself because it leads to thinking and paying attention. Thinking is part of reading and comprehending. To understand, you must focus and pay attention to details. They do not want you to be nosy because then you will think, reason, and draw your own conclusions to solve your own problems. You have to remember that what your mind takes in from observing and reading is what you use to make decisions. All of us must be nosy to learn. And we must become involved in our own business, just as we are in everyone else's, to learn who and what we are and our responsibility as humans. Being nosy helps you to think, challenges you to know more, and forces you to process the knowledge you learn. A person who is nosy is actually naturally smart and has just put too much focus on other people's lives rather than on himself or herself.

Most of the time, many of us do not know we are being nosy about other people until someone else brings it to our attention. Without knowing it, nosy people are practicing psychology. Psychology is the study of human behavior—what people do, how they think, and how they make choices. No one has ever said that about a nosy person. Usually, we are told, "Stop being so nosy." We don't know how to apply nosiness in our own life because we have been told it is not right to do that.

We have been told not to gossip, but we have not been told how a nosy person can use nosiness to become successful—in a career as a psychiatrist, interrogator, detective, judge, lawyer, or any profession that requires thinking about and solving other people's problems by studying their behavior and choices. For instance, a criminal detective deals primarily with studying how people act. Afterward, the detective uses that information and information about the choices people make, draws conclusions, and then tries to solve a case.

In a different light, what detectives, police officers, and others are typically doing is profiling. Profiling is using a person's history of behavior, traits, and observed characteristics to understand what they are capable of doing or have done. People in law enforcement use profiling to prevent crime. Psychiatrists use the same approach to help solve people's mental problems. Every jury and judge does this to determine if a person is guilty or innocent. We all do it. All of this deals with science, social science, political science, investigation, and more.

Because no one is asking real questions, people are not solving their own problems and using history to understand them. The idea here is that you have to be nosy about yourself and your surroundings to change the future and take advantage of the many opportunities that come with it.

When you are in school or business, people tell you not to discuss politics and religion, mainly because they do not want you thinking and snooping around looking for answers; they are afraid you might figure out what they are doing. They do not want you thinking and talking about religion and politics because they want to talk about and snoop into your life. It is like having a corrupt leader or a community activist telling you not to listen to people whose views are opposite theirs. Why? Do these people know something about the leader or activist that he or she does not want you to know? You have to be nosy about politics and religion. They influence societies and cultures; they are important parts of life.

Be mindful. Anytime people tell you not to do something, think first, be logical, do your research, compare what you find with your values, and then ask yourself, *What would God want me to do?* Nine times out ten, He would want us to talk, gossip, and be nosy with others and ourselves to gain knowledge and use mind over matter. As I said earlier, the word *knowledge* has two parts, *know* and *ledge*, or we can say *now* and *edge*, which mean exactly what they appear to mean. To know is to become aware. The part *now* means "at this moment in time." The words *ledge* and *edge* describe the end or the outside limit of something.

NINE

Have a Dream

Your dreams are in your mind, stored in the hope that you one day can turn them into reality. There are images and pieces of knowledge in your dreams that are clues to what you can foresee to accomplish. We dream in our sleep, and we daydream while we are awake, but both dreaming and daydreaming are simply ideas about you.

You Are Your Dreams

Dreams are collections of images, emotions, and thoughts that pass through our minds night and day. They are constant reminders of what is coming up so we can better prepare ourselves for the future. Dreams are desires from our deepest thoughts that help us picture possibilities, survive, and adapt in everyday surroundings. Dreams are the part of our imagination that helps us create pictures to go with our thoughts. They give us insights and clues to our future; they are the interpretation of our human reality. Dreams are a part of our human experience, and we need them to help us get ahead in life. What is in our dreams is in us—our present, past, and future.

Dreams let us see what we can do; they show us how gifted and talented we are when placed in difficult situations. Because of this, there is nothing we cannot do. We were made to unravel complicated things and solve the hardest of problems. Dreams train us to prepare for the unknown and for things we do not understand. They give us the strength to face our fears. Not all fear is bad. It helps us to become prepared and aware of the unknown. Without dreams, we are without hope and the confidence to picture how great we can become. Dreams are how the Creator communicates with us spiritually. Dreams test our faith to see which path we choose. Dreaming helps us face our fears before we engage in reality. Those images in our dreams help us understand our purpose so we can see the pathway of our journey, one that often leads to success or, at least, allows us to decide our own future and define our past. Once we put the right one in place, there is no telling what we can achieve.

Our dreams ignite our confidence, give us courage, and light the fuse of our rocket to success. Dreaming helps us see what is possible, which comes from what we believe, worship, and focus on. Nothing is possible if there is no power in your belief. Belief is the sole foundation upon which we build to make our dreams come true. Those dreams are the prototypes of our ideas, and with faith, they become exactly what we hope our dreams look like when we bring them to life. Afterward, when we have made our dreams real, perfectly altered them, and seen what we can do, the magic begins. At that moment, we are the producer of our dreams, the director of our thoughts, and the stars of our future. With faith, we are the dream.

The I *in* We

They say, "There is no *I* in the word *we*," but I say, "In *we*, there are a whole bunch of *Is*." However, each individual has his or her own type of *we*—the me, myself, and I—and without complete knowledge of them, there is no *I* for any team. Every *I* in *we* and *team* has to take care of himself or herself and his or her family. To serve any team, you must be right with yourself. Your mind must have a focus, your body must be healthy, strong, fresh, and good, and your soul must be filled with good morals.

On every sports team, only one dream prevails: the dream of the owner. Players on the team have their own dreams they have wished for and realized in a certain amount of fame and fortune while trying to advance to the next stage in their lives. That next step might be another job or a position on another team, so their plan would be to move on to what they believe is better. If they do not find what is better, they stay where they are. But their dreams do not matter when compared with the owner's dream. No matter what happens, the *I* is the owner, who will always try to keep his team, the *we*, together with the team's many *Is*.

The idea here is that you must get yourself together before you can work as a team. Although the *we* in team is important, the *I* in you is just as important, for it is controlled by you. Every year, teams change as some players leave and new ones arrive, so never forget the *I* and the *we* within you. There is nothing more important than you, which is why no two people are alike.

An important team that has helped you become who and what you are is made up of your family and friends. They have stuck by you and believed in you when you could not see the dream in you. They helped you along when there was no one else, showed you opportunities when there was no hope left. So never forget the *I* in the *we* of your family and friends.

Have a goal and make sure yours is met while playing on the team. A player without a plan of his or her own or without another option will fail. You must prepare yourself and control your destiny. If living your dream through others is part of your plan, make sure your plan includes options in case you have to leave. Play the game if you want. Just know that in the end you are an individual talent who joined the *we* to get rich or advance the *I* in you.

Have a Dream

Everyone must have a dream controlled by the self and received from his or her experiences and education. When we work for someone, we are not quite in control of our dreams. We are under the control of others; we are working, dreaming our dream, and using our skills within someone else's dream.

To be fair, working for others can be great when it pays you well. But working a job can be a training course before branching out on your own. You are hired to perform a task at a certain time each day, and the job may rely on very little of your brain and your thinking. But when you gain the knowledge and skills to own a business, you are responsible for everything and must use your whole brain. As owner of a business, you are the manager and the organizer of the entire operation. You control the inside of your business, as well as that business within yourself. Have a dream of your own and become the owner of a business.

Every player must dream of owning a team, even if he or she never achieves it. Dreaming helps prepare the mind to see what could be next in one's life and what is possible. Dreams keep us imagining and planning for a greater future, a better life, and better equip us for our journey.

Imagine being a member of a sports team. It is really the dream of the team's owner that is being manifested; the players are just living their dreams within the owner's. The players become part of the owner's dream of having a team. Every year, players are drafted and become part of an owner's dream—his or her plan. The owner, with the help of his or her staff, especially the coaches, decides what position each player will play and what tasks each player is best suited to perform in the owner's dream. They decide how much to pay the players for their performance and contribution to the owner's dream and how long players can receive that payment. But when you own the dream, you decide its future. In other words, put a limit on how long you will work in someone else's dream, until you are ready to live your own dream as an owner.

As you work in another's dream, you have no need for an attitude. Instead, show gratitude and feed your dream with the experience and education you are receiving. Any business owner cares about you and the other employees, but you are not the focus; the business is the focus, just as it would be if the business were your dream. An owner must stay ahead of his or her competitors. Education and a paycheck help you grow, but good business decisions and investments help an owner grow. Owners must make sure everything is intact and in order, running smoothly, bringing in money, keeping customers happy, and more. The owner decides the value of the entire business. The employees have value, as long as the owner needs them to make the business a success. Their value is determined by their performance, which is where they control their dream. At the end of the day, every business owner expects his or her dream to become real, for the business to become the best. Understand, the owner is building his legacy and for it to be passed down to his children, he must make himself and his business memorable.

Partnering Dreams

There is nothing wrong with having a partner as part of your dream, as long as you are not the only active partner. The purpose of having a partner is to receive help to advance you or your business to the next level. That help must consist of knowledge, financial support, time, or other resources that can change the scope of your business instantly and correctly. Effective knowledge received with resources can elevate you quickly and give you another perspective on growing the business. Money will open many closed doors, get quicker responses, and buy so-called friends who will do anything to be part of something successful. People will give you their time and bring you followers who will help and support everything you do, which will produce that success over and over again.

If your personal business has a partner who cannot give you at least one of the three—knowledge, financial support, or time—you are essentially giving your business away for free. You are one person away from failing. Do not waste your time with people who are worthless to your cause, your dream. No one needs to be held back because of unnecessary baggage. You do not need a partner for show or to make you feel good; anyone can have that. What your personal business needs most is to thrive, so focus on that. Do not get caught with a partner who will make your business look bad and possibly fail; you can do that on your own. Failure has never needed help but will comfort those who are used to failing and expect to see it in you. There is certainly no need to have a partner who has nothing to offer you. The idea of a partnership is to help you build your dream into a successful empire, not to tear it down just as it is getting started.

When you bring partners into a relationship, you are doing so to grow and prosper. But with most Americans lacking knowledge, partners who can really help are difficult to find. Never do business with family and friends who lack business experience or correct knowledge and thinking. Their knowledge must be deeply rooted in experience in business (especially your type of business) before they can help your personal business bloom. Let them fail on their own and then succeed before you offer them the opportunity to partner with you. Play every role in your dream and perform every task until you find what you are best at. Then fill in the blanks with others who have the knowledge you need or can make up for where you are weak. Be careful because those sharing your dream can become rivals if you don't pay attention.

TEN

Gifts and Talents

A genius is someone with great natural intellectual ability, creativity, and originality. The first signs of genius are in the mother's womb. Each of us is gifted, talented, and skillful, and because no two of us are exactly alike, each is an original, a one-of-a-kind.

Genius in You

Every one of us was born a genius, smart, and intelligent, but the scientist in us makes each one of us unique and special. All of us are born from greatness, created by the greatest scientist, mathematician, and teacher in the history of this universe. We are all images of God, created with a scientific mind-set to invent, create, discover, enhance, and make difficult things simpler in order to progress and evolve. There is nothing that we cannot do. Everything you think you need, you already have. You inherited it! We are our greatest asset and investment, more important than anything we could ever imagine. Open your eyes to see your greatness. Your purpose is to grow, teach, prosper, produce life, and use your individual gifts to explore life and your greatness. But first, you must know who you are.

There are two types of gifted and successful people: those who are destined to succeed and those who are determined to succeed. Those who are destined are given the opportunity to recognize their gifts at a very early age, so they do not have any excuse for not knowing and discovering their purpose. Those who are determined to succeed are given more time to uncover their gifts to learn how to use them and make the best life. These individuals are self-motivated and refuse to give up, even if success is not necessarily part of their destiny.

Every one of us in this world has a purpose and was born with a gift, talent, or some type of unique ability. But to use our gifts, we must recognize what they are. Even if you are short in height or big in weight, you can use your size as a gift to your advantage. Talking is a talent for many, and so are eating, reading, and writing. Other special skills are in how we use things around us, the speed with which we make things happen, and how we make them happen so that other great things can occur. It is up to each one of us to understand who we are, our differences, why we were created or exist, and what makes us special—our gifts, talents, and unique skills—to create the best future. We can achieve a greater understanding of ourselves by putting aside time to reflect on our lives, our purpose, and our place here in this world. We have to talk to ourselves and ask ourselves questions about the many choices we have made from our experiences and learn from them. Try to explore things that may or may not spark your interest but can open up many possibilities. Write down what you like or dislike about things you have experienced and then pursue those things that come easily for you. Meditation is another technique. It can help us become more focused, calm, and patient, and to concentrate. I am not saying it's going to be easy, but through trying, studying, and practicing continually with repeated efforts, you will be fine. Most of us may share the same ideas and the same dreams, and that is okay. Not all of us do the same things or do them in the same way, but that is the beauty of our uniqueness. If everyone were the same, how would we be unique? We are all different in our own way, but that is what makes us great together. We just have to keep striving to get better, to become a better person, better nation, better culture, and better community.

Discovering Greatness

Life has many stages, and during some that we pass through, we discover more about ourselves and the ways in which we should live. The path that leads to the greatest good lies in our Creator, from whom we receive our beliefs. When we were born or came into existence, we possessed or were given some of the greatest gifts—a good life and love—as well as special skills. Every time we use these gifts, we prosper, and every time we apply them, we grow, flourish, expand, and become what all of us are intended to become: successful in His image.

Most of all, we should know that we were given these gifts, talents, and unique abilities to serve the Creator and to help each other prosper. A genius is creative and gifted, as we all are. Whenever a genius achieves greatness, nothing can compare to it, and there is no competition. Evil people hate greatness if they cannot claim it first. Geniuses thrive where there are problems and there is love, encouragement, and hope. A genius is unique, starting from the first days of existence and in all areas of life— food, medicine, knowledge, vision, humanity, fashion, faith, and color. It is our assignment to be good stewards of all we have been given and to contribute to life for everyone's benefit. I cannot tell you what to do with your gift or what your purpose is, but I do know that all of us were born a genius, gifted with senses, creative abilities, tools, and powers to think and act with love.

We have to stop looking in the mirror at just the reflection and look more deeply at the true beauty within ourselves. Some people do not know what they see in the mirror. Open your eyes and see who you are. How can we look in the mirror every day but never see the gifts the Creator has given us from birth? We were born to prosper, to expand our scientific knowledge, and to create new ideas or goods or services to improve our lives. We were born with the gift of greatness for our mothers and fathers to develop, nurture, and guide. These skills and talents are for you to use and share with the world to provide a better life for all. The Creator gave us our gifts, and without Him we cannot prosper.

If it had not been for the Creator's grace, how would you have known at the moment of birth that you would survive? How would you have known the moment you exited the womb to take your first breath without being told? And a few months later, how would you have known that your arms were strong enough to crawl without anyone else's example to imitate? How else could you have known that your legs were strong enough to stand and to walk? You even knew to walk without help. And when you wanted something, you knew to laugh and cry to get it without knowing what an emotion is and why emotions are useful.

Because many of us have not been taught that we were born with great abilities, we have not used them to take us further. Stop holding on to your gifts and let them go so you can have the greatest life.

The greatest gift is the need to seek the Creator so He can show you your path. Success is within reach. Keep reaching. Make them remember you! Live your legacy! There is a genius living within you waiting to come out. Many have been told that America or someone owes them. Not true. You owe yourself. Show your receipt; your greatness proves you have already received it. Some are convinced that success comes only in one color, but there are many. Pick the color that best suits you and mimic it the best way you know how. Otherwise, do not get caught in a room without your gift or the knowledge that you have the power within you to unwrap it and use it. In the end, your gift will make your sleep sweet and rich in all areas of life.

What We Possess

We all possess the greatest gift: love. Love is more powerful than hate or any amount of money. It is the gift of all gifts; without love, we are nothing to others or ourselves. But putting too much love into others can cause you to lose focus and follow their gifts instead of yours. Many of us have not been taught we have a gift, because it brings happiness to a deceiver. Through love, all things are made possible. How can you have faith in the Creator but not follow His laws? As long as you are seriously trying, you will prosper. Faith without love is just faith with no effort. The Creator blesses us when we choose to love Him, others, and ourselves. Many of us do not even try because we are afraid of losing and do not love ourselves. Many have lived vicariously through others' successes because they didn't love themselves. Strive for your own greatness. Once you can apply love to all things—your confidence, your ambition, and your efforts—you will see your destiny fulfilled in front of your very own eyes.

There are many things you must understand about your gift and your purpose. God did not create you so you would abandon your mind, gifts, talents, and unique abilities, and He surely did not create you to beg and wait on others for a handout. Control your destiny. What makes America so great is that each one of us can use our creative abilities to become whatever we want and strive for the greatest and highest goals. Pay no attention to bad leadership that changed our course and altered our destiny.

Our biggest problem has been the past—slavery, oppression, racism, and political corruption. But none of these things has anything to do with you succeeding now, except political corruption, and you can change that by knowing how to recognize the deceivers. Their past is not your past, nor is it your future. No effort can make you repeat a painful past if you get up and make something happen now. Make them remember you. Live your legacy now. If your ancestors' past has hindered your future because you have refused to be independent, leave that past behind. That past will not help you in the future. Someone you have never had contact with cannot affect you. And you cannot suffer from a place if you've never been there. Do not let your gifts slip away because you are so caught up in the past that you refuse to develop and use them. Think! Too many of us have not found our gifts so we have failed to enhance our lives by following our dreams and living up to our legacy. All of us have natural gifts, but we have to let them work to allow our greatness to take its course.

Setting Goals

Without a set goal, there can be no true success. And a goal set by others cannot be your goal; each person must have his or her own goal. Goals set within the perimeter of God's laws will benefit all humankind. The opposite is also true; if an individual's goals are destructive (outside God's laws), then all society will suffer. A person without an individual goal will eventually become a burden to others, and dependency will again prevail. No plan, no goal; no goal, no hope. People without a plan have nothing by which to measure their growth. Dreams well planned will create wealth in all areas of one's life. Having wealth is not always the result of robbing the poor; most people who become wealthy plan and work for their success. It is of great importance to write down our goals and objectives. That allows us to tap into the creative areas of our brain. Most successful people write down their plans, which enables them to envision their success. They make a conscious effort to periodically update and reevaluate their plans, objectives, and progress.

No genuine success is accidental; it must be planned. With planning comes awareness and readiness to succeed. You do not need a plan to fail, but you do need a plan to succeed. Planning is the best foundation for confidence.

Prepare for Failure

From the minute we are born, failure looks for those who are not ready or have not prepared themselves. It looks for those who seem as if they have been rejected and turned down or as if they have been struggling. Many people remain in their comfort zones because they are afraid of change that comes when we venture outside of those zones. Fear of failure keeps us from pursuing our dreams. Failure looks for those who do not understand or know things, but with truth, preparation will always repel failure and evil. Some people pray that the failure will go away. But praying is not all you have; trying is all you have left. Our lack of trying will not advance us; it will just keep adding on more failures, more discomfort, and more problems. The more you try, the closer you'll get to success. Just be consistent. Stay the course, no matter how much pressure you feel. With truth, there is no failure. No one can force you to turn left when you know to turn right.

To correct a problem, you must be aware of it. But you do not necessarily need to decide on a plan before working on the problem; just do what you love, and success will come. A child writing in a journal may not be aware of a plan at first, but later he or she may become the author of a life-changing book. As long as you keep searching, you will find it. The idea is to take one day at a time, stay focused, and live your legacy.

Be Courageous

David knew that Goliath was a giant, but David did not care, because he trusted in God's help more than he feared his enemy. As David knew, having courage does not mean an encounter will be easy. It just means you will not stand for anything holding you back anymore because your problem will just get bigger if you wait till tomorrow to deal with it. Truth gives strength to courage. When you know truth is in sight, your plan will last. We need the same type of courage David showed in his battle with Goliath to stand on the things we truly believe in.

Thinking we do not have something is caused by believing that we cannot have it. We have to push ourselves past the knowledge limits we have set for ourselves. Many people have been fed wrong ideas and wrong attitudes about their lives. Too often we are trapped in fear of ourselves because we choose not to understand the game that is being played on us. That is like playing football all your life and later deciding to take a paying job as a soccer coach; it will never work. Life and learning do not come easily; they always come with a price. Working to get paid is one of life's challenges, but you need training before you are ready for most jobs.

The mind must be focused. It was created that way and will find a point of focus, whether that point is good or bad. There is nothing that we cannot do when our minds are focused on worthy goals. There is something special about all of us—black, white, and brown. We are all human beings, born for greatness, created by the greatest scientist, the Creator of the universe, to be the most important species on this planet. We are the only species that has so many unique capabilities and talents. We have the ability to change things for the better, and we can do things just to show they can be done. Each of us has a purpose; through God's love and strength, we are able to fulfill it.

The past is behind us; the truth stands out in front. It is here where we put away the blame game and see that this country is full of possibilities and opportunities for us. The Creator loves us and wants us to succeed as long as we love one another and ourselves. He created us to succeed. Why do we hold ourselves back from succeeding? Why do we try to destroy our chances?

No longer should we let fear or false pride or ignorance lead us astray when the truth is right in front of us. Truth and knowledge are part of a creative life lived in God's love. Nothing exists that holds more possibilities for a creative life than truth. Truth, reality, creativity, love, and success are all part of God's plan for our lives. When you know it in your deepest self, you can become passionate about using your talents to create a happy and fulfilling life. Open yourself to the possibilities the Creator gives us in this life, succeed in creating the best you, and help your family do the same.

Know the Challenges

There will be many obstacles and challenges in life, so it is best to know yourself. Everyone has a weakness, and some have suffered from their weaknesses. But all of us also have the strength to change our lives and achieve success. To make that transition, we must be able to recognize the difference between weakness and strength. Time and research have proved that if you know your history, you can one day find your strength and your purpose. Your history consists of your experiences and past events. Just remember your history starts at home. Using your strength is the only answer to overcoming obstacles. Children who are raised by single parents need to know their parents' histories to find their journeys. Knowing history creates a strong foundation of growth and understanding so you can avoid making the mistakes of the past in similar situations today.

There will be many obstacles and barriers in each of our lives. Reading our ancestors' diaries and letters about how they handled their troubles helps us understand we are not alone in any difficulty. We realize others have gone through similar problems and survived and were the better for it. It is up to us to find the strength and courage we need to discover our dreams and purpose. Every moment we waste postpones our fulfillment. Without strength and belief and effort, we fail to see our imagination turn into reality. We have faced so many setbacks and so many consequences from our wrong choices that we have lost sight of our future. Our poor choices, our confusion, and our disillusionment have caused us to picture life as hopeless. But we can elevate ourselves by continuing to grow and learn about others and ourselves. Life entails a process of growth. Either we choose to lose ourselves to all hope, moving downward toward death, or we choose to be a creative part of life, moving upward in hope.

Imagine everything in your life as a list of obstacles and challenges that have tested your ability to grow and prosper. Every obstacle and challenge can make you stronger and wiser and a winner, or you can give in to defeat, hopelessness, and death. The Creator promises to give you the strength you need to overcome any obstacle and promises you will never be tested beyond your ability to endure. There is no need for fear where there is love and faith.

So imagine yourself in your everyday life, waking up with certain challenges that all of us have sooner or later. We fight for what we want and what we believe in, whether it is in the past, present, or future. If you have an issue with children, finances, a job, or even your health, accept that it is your responsibility to deal with it with God's guaranteed help. Make them remember you! Live your legacy! You cannot continue to be trapped inside yourself, afraid to grow and improve your life. If you are a parent, you serve a greater purpose in helping your children deal with their own obstacles in growing up. Part of your daily assignment is to guide them through their challenges. You have daily opportunities to teach them how to face their problems with courage, grow from their experiences, and gradually take more and more responsibility for their own lives.

All of us are responsible for finding fulfillment, discovering ourselves, growing as we face our challenges, and knowing that the Creator provides us with whatever we need to succeed as long as we are not going against His will. As the purpose of each obstacle and opportunity is for personal growth, the purpose of one job is for your professional growth—to train yourself for the next level, becoming a manager and then CEO of a company or owner of your own business. A job is only a step that you must take to get to your final destination because the only way you will appreciate success is to know how you got there. What you learn in your journey strengthens and prepares you for the next challenging opportunity. To succeed in life, you must find your talent and follow it, for that is your gift. Use it to feed yourself and your family.

Finally, you must understand that we were born out of greatness. We are geniuses, scientists, mathematicians, historians, and authors with great abilities, but maintaining our greatness requires that we explore and put our skills to work. Exploring means doing work and showing action to educate ourselves and learn things. We have five known senses and our minds and should use them. We do not need an institution to validate who we are or what our purpose is.

One key to succeeding is to go back and examine everything that has been taught to you. Separate those things that have hindered you from those that have helped you. Then discard what did not help and do more of what did help. To uncover the truth, to get the correct answers, and to know, we must think, try, act, read, ask questions, talk, and research. We are expected to do more with our lives. There is absolutely nothing to be afraid of. Understand there will be many successes and failures; be prepared to experience plenty of each. The idea is to learn from your mistakes so you will not be afraid and ashamed of failing.

Our lives are all on us, so embrace the positive. Live life in the Creator's love, and have the courage to be the special person you are already. Find out who you are, and learn to live the legacy that has been left just for you. Make them remember you before its too late. Change the game!

NOTES

1. https://www.encyclopedia.com/social-sciences-and-law/sociology-and-social-reform/sociology-general-terms-and-concepts/single-parent-families.
2. https://www.datacenter.kidcount.org.
3. https://www.afro.com/census-bureau-higher-percentage-black-children-live-single-mothers/.
4. http://www.chicagotribune.com/ct-youth-unemployment-urban-league-0126-biz-20160124-story.html.
5. https://www.pbs.org/newshour/education/high-school-grads-may-not-be-college-ready.
6. https://www.dailymail.co.uk/news/article-3405298/Exclusive-rare-audio-recording-Dr-King-s-1964-Nobel-Peace-Prize-lecture-calls-end-mankind-s-evils-racial-injustice-poverty-war-echo-famous-Dream-speech.html.

CPSIA information can be obtained
at www.ICGtesting.com
Printed in the USA
BVHW051543040319
541706BV00022B/1301/P